BRONZE
METAL CLAY

BRONZE
METAL CLAY

Explore a New Material with 35 Projects

YVONNE M. PADILLA

An Imprint of Sterling Publishing Co., Inc.
New York

WWW.LARKCRAFTS.COM

Editor:
Linda Kopp

Art Director:
Megan Kirby

Layout and Production:
828:design

**How-to Illustrations
and Templates:**
James Gros

Photography Director:
Dana Irwin

Photographer:
Stewart O'Shields

Cover Designer:
Chris Bryant

Library of Congress Cataloging-in-Publication Data

Padilla, Yvonne M.
  Bronze metal clay : explore a new material with 35 projects / Yvonne M. Padilla.
     p. cm.
  Includes index.
  ISBN 978-1-60059-463-2 (pb-trade pbk. : alk. paper)
  1. Metal-work. 2. Bronze. 3. Precious metal clay. I. Title.
  TT213.P33 2010
  684'.09--dc22

                                        2009037359

10 9 8 7 6 5 4 3 2

Published by Lark Crafts, An Imprint of
Sterling Publishing Co., Inc.
387 Park Avenue South, New York, NY 10016

Text © 2010, Yvonne M. Padilla
Project Sketches © 2010, Yvonne M. Padilla
Photography © 2010, Lark Crafts, An Imprint of Sterling Publishing Co., Inc., unless otherwise specified
Illustrations © 2010, Lark Crafts, An Imprint of Sterling Publishing Co., Inc., unless otherwise specified

Distributed in Canada by Sterling Publishing,
c/o Canadian Manda Group, 165 Dufferin Street
Toronto, Ontario, Canada M6K 3H6

Distributed in the United Kingdom by GMC Distribution Services,
Castle Place, 166 High Street, Lewes, East Sussex, England BN7 1XU

Distributed in Australia by Capricorn Link (Australia) Pty Ltd.,
P.O. Box 704, Windsor, NSW 2756 Australia

If you have questions or comments about this book, please contact:
Lark Crafts
67 Broadway
Asheville, NC 28801
828-253-0467

Manufactured in China

ISBN 13: 978-1-60059-463-2

For information about custom editions, special sales, premium and corporate purchases, please contact
Sterling Special Sales Department at 800-805-5489 or specialsales@sterlingpub.com.

For information about desk and examination copies available to college and university professors,
requests must be submitted to academic@larkbooks.com. Our complete policy can be found
at www.larkcrafts.com.

CONTENTS

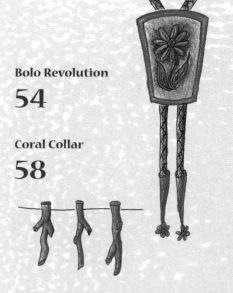

Bolo Revolution
54

Coral Collar
58

Coasters del Sol
60

Mosaic Bracelet
34

Juliet Earrings
44

Milagro Charms
62

Ancient Treasures
37

Arrowhead Pendant
47

Evolution Hoops
64

Corona Pendant
40

Tribeca Belt Buckle
50

Serpentine Ring
66

Hacienda Numbers
42

Illumination Vessel
52

Mayan Hoops
69

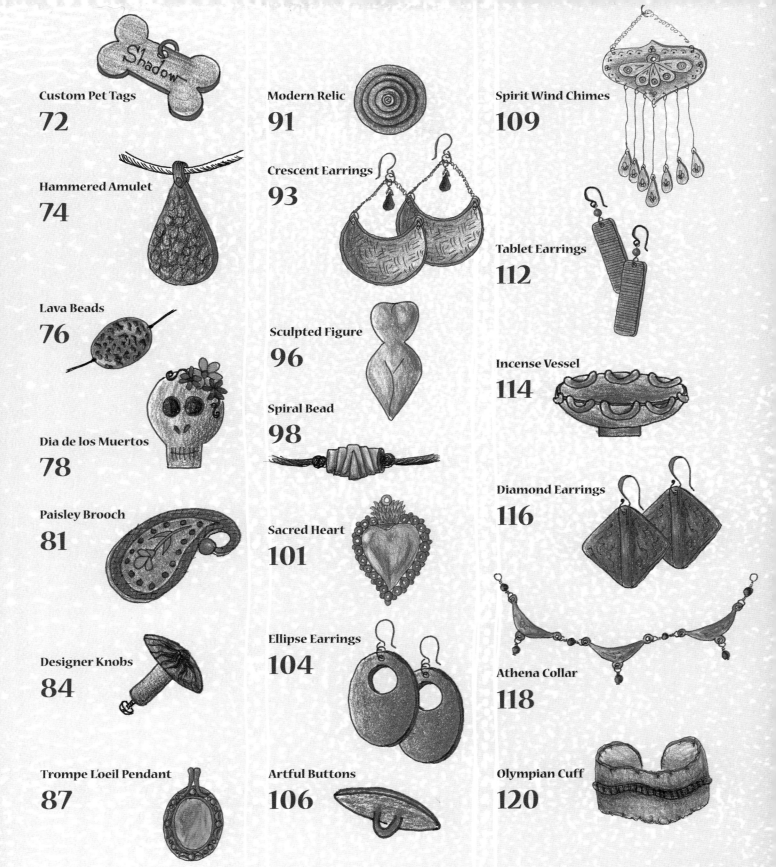

INTRODUCTION

When I was a kid, I loved any type of arts and crafts project. I had the BIG box of crayons, wove friendship bracelets constantly, and was always on my mom's sewing machine making funny little pillows and stuffed toys. But the thing I loved the most was playing with clay. Play-dough was cool, but I found it limiting since it only came in a few colors and in such small jars. To solve that problem, I began to make my own clay out of salt and flour—salt dough.

As I got older, I drifted away from clay, but I still dabbled with every medium I could get my hands on. In my early twenties, I discovered polymer clay. Although it was different than the salt dough of my childhood, working with it took me back to those long hours I spent in the kitchen making my own clay.

And then the world of clay changed. In 1996, silver metal clay made its debut. I was awestruck! I could use the same tools, the same motions, and the same ideas to create a piece of metal jewelry. It's hard to describe the thrill I felt when I realized I could take a piece of clay and make something so beautiful and wearable.

Fast forward a few years, and we have the newest addition to the metal clay family—bronze clay. Bronze clay is an exciting new material that gives you options that aren't possible or practical with other types of metal clay. Because it's so affordable, you can experiment with different designs without fear of "wasting it." Also, because of its affordability, you can work big! For example, check out Coasters del Sol (page 60), Hacienda Numbers (page 42), and Spirit Wind Chime (page 109).

But as with transitioning from polymer clay to silver metal clay, there is a slight learning curve with this new material. Because bronze clay is a mixture of two metals—copper and tin—it behaves differently than silver or gold metal clay. So, take your time and get to know the clay.

In this book, we'll discuss the basics of working with the clay as well as some intermediate and advanced techniques. I'll also address frequently asked questions about using and working with the clay.

Bronze clay is a new medium with a huge potential that's just starting to be tapped. Every time I work with it I learn something new. So I encourage you, my fellow artists, to join in the fun and be a pioneer with bronze clay. You're going to love it!

BRONZE
METAL CLAY
BASICS

Bronze clay is an exciting new medium that draws both beginners as well as experienced metal clay artists. Although the cost of the clay is inexpensive when compared to silver or gold metal clay, there are other costs involved. Bronze clay must be fired in a kiln, so you need to keep that in mind if you're just getting started. Along with a kiln you'll need activated carbon and a firing container.

Even though beginners can easily use bronze clay, this book focuses on several intermediate and advanced metal clay techniques. There are lots of fantastic books available that discuss the basics of using silver metal clay.

I've had the good fortune of being one of the first artists to help test bronze clay. This is just a portion of my job, which is supplying technical support to the customers of Rio Grande. One of the best things about my position is that I get to teach LOTS of classes about metal clay. Yes, I get to play with clay and talk about making jewelry for a living. Life is good! Since bronze metal clay is a new material, I get a lot of questions about it. Here I'm sharing the answers to the most frequently asked questions I encounter on a daily basis. Enjoy!

NISA SMILEY
Bronze Lantern Bells, 2008
2.5 to 3.8 cm in diameter
Bronze clay; patina, carved, fired
Photo by Robert Diamante

CELIE FAGO
Abacus Ring, 2008
3.2 x 2.8 cm
Bronze clay, river stones, diamonds, red brass, sterling silver; formed, heat patina, riveted
Photo by Douglas Foulke

Is working with bronze clay the same as silver clay?

There are as many similarities as there are differences between bronze and silver clay. Bronze clay will feel slightly stiff when you remove it from the package. The clay is easier to work if you knead it first, before you start working with it. To do this, just press the clay between your fingers to flatten it and then fold it onto itself. After folding the clay, press the clay in the center and work your way to the edges. This will help to eliminate any trapped air bubbles. If air bubbles become trapped, press them out with your fingers or use a needle tool to cut into the clay and release the air. After you've finished kneading the clay, place it back into the original packaging or wrap it in plastic wrap, and let it sit for a minute or two. This will help dissipate any body heat that may have transferred from your hands to the clay, which can cause the clay to tighten.

The binder in bronze clay works best when it's cool, so you may want to place the clay in the fridge before working with it. Overworking the clay sometimes makes it start to feel stiff. If this happens, place the clay in plastic wrap or in a plastic zipper bag, and let it sit for a few minutes to allow it to cool down and relax. You can also place it back into the refrigerator to help it cool faster.

Because bronze clay is water based, it can feel a little sticky once you start working with it. To prevent it from sticking, rub your hands and tools with a bit of olive oil or one of the commercially made releases that is designed specifically for use with metal clay. It's important to stay away from anything that's petroleum or silicone based; these products won't burn away cleanly and can cause problems with sintering.

Bronze clay has elasticity to it that silver clay doesn't. As you're working with bronze clay, you may find that it stretches slightly. Use a light touch when handling the clay to avoid distortion. When cutting, the clay may stick to your cutting blade. If this happens, gently lift the blade out of the clay slowly to avoid excessively distorting it. Another thing to keep in mind is that once fired, bronze clay shrinks about 20 percent in size.

PATRIK KUSEK
Cuff, **2008**
6 x 11 cm
Bronze clay; custom textures
Photo by artist

BARBARA BECKER SIMON
Lemon Wedge Bead, **2008**
5 x 2 cm
Bronze clay, diamond; hollow construction
Photo by Larry Sanders

11

DAWN WILSON-ENOCH
Ritual Effect, 2008
Ring, 6.3 x 5 x 0.4 cm
Necklace, 50 cm long
Bronze clay; patina, fired, hand finished
Photo by Margot Geist

GAIL LANNUM
Ugarit Shield, 2009
4.5 cm in diameter
Bronze clay
Photo by artist

I work with silver metal clay. Can I use the same tools with bronze clay?

Yes, lots of the same tools can be used between silver clay and bronze clay. I use stamps and texture with both clays, but I make sure that they are completely clean before switching clay types. When it comes to the tools that I use often—such as a rolling pin, cutting blades, and paintbrushes—or ones that are hard to clean, I have a dedicated set for each type of clay that I'm using.

If you do use the same tools for both bronze and silver clays, you need to make sure that the tools are completely clean before going from one type of clay to the other. If the tools aren't totally clean, you run the risk of contaminating the clay. If pieces of bronze clay, even the dust, get mixed into silver clay, you'll notice black specks in the silver. These specks are the bronze that has become oxidized during firing. If silver clay gets mixed into the bronze, the silver won't sinter (the process of heating the particles of metal until they stick to each other). The silver pieces will eventually become dislodged, leaving small voids in the bronze.

BRONZE CLAY TOOL KIT
To make many of the projects in this book, besides bronze clay, you'll need the items listed below.

Work surface

Olive oil or other lubricant

Rolling pin

Playing cards/risers

Blending tool

Thin paintbrush

Spray bottle for water

Craft knife

Nail files, assorted grits

Fiber sanding pad

400-grit sand paper

Needle tool

Tissue blade

Polishing cloth

Drying tray or food dehydrator

What types of bronze clay products are currently available?

Whereas other types of metal clay come in various forms such as slip, paste, or sheet, bronze clay only comes in lump form. The clay is available in 100- or 200-gram packages, so there's plenty of clay to make your own slip or paste.

The package sizes that bronze clay is sold in are pretty large. How do I store my unused clay?

Unopened packages of bronze clay can be stored at room temperature or in the refrigerator. The clay is vacuum-sealed inside a plastic zipper bag and then sealed in a second foil bag. Since it's packaged in two bags, the clay will remain workable for several months. Each project in this book can be made with 100 grams or less of clay (except for Coasters del Sol where you need 150 grams for a set of four).

Once the package has been opened, it's best to store the unused clay in the fridge. Keep the unused portion of clay in a sealed plastic zipper bag. Sometimes I end up with several open packages. To keep them all centrally located, I put them in a plastic bowl with a tight-fitting lid. If I don't expect to use the clay for several days, I also place a clean, damp sponge in the bowl. This keeps the air in the bowl moist, thus preventing the clay from drying out. I keep the bowl in my refrigerator until I'm ready to use the clay. It's a good idea to label the bowl so everyone else in your house knows that it's being used to store bronze clay and not last night's leftovers.

At times, you may see the clay turn slightly moldy or discolored. This isn't a problem. Simply use a craft knife to scrape away any discoloration. If there's any mold remaining on the clay, it'll burn away during firing.

I've heard that you should use lavender oil when working with bronze clay. Why?

You can add lavender oil directly to the bronze clay. This helps keep the clay moist and supple while you're working with it. It also helps to inhibit oxidation from forming on the clay as it's being used.

DAWN WILSON-ENOCH
Ancient Surfaces, 2009
7 x 2 x 0.2 cm
Bronze clay; patina, fired, hand finished
Photo by Margot Geist

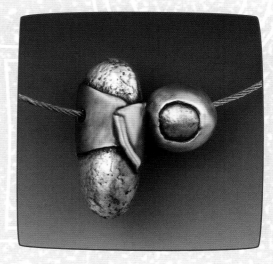

HADAR JACOBSON
Rods, 2008
Largest, 4 x 2 x 1 cm
Bronze clay, silver clay; fired
Photo by artist

13

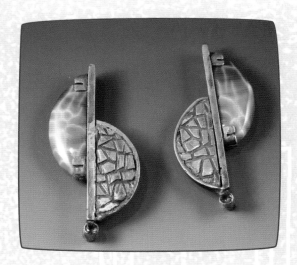

SANDRA GRAVES
Textures, 2008
5 x 3 x 1.8 cm
Bronze clay, copper bezel, copper tube,
garnet, sterling silver, carnelian agate
cabochon; fired, soldered
Cut by Gary Wilson
Photo by artist

TERRY KOVALCIK
Seed Pod Earrings, 2008
7.6 x 1.5 x 1.5 cm
Bronze clay, liver of sulphur; sculpted,
carved hollow form, patina
Photo by Corrin Jacobsen Kovalcik

You can also add one or two drops of the oil to your water dish to use when you're rehydrating the clay or making slip. I keep lavender water in my spray bottle. When the clay is sprayed, a small amount of lavender oil is left on the surface, protecting it from oxidizing.

Lavender oil water will keep for several days. Eventually some clay will build up in the bottom of the water dish. You may notice the bronze in the water dish becoming discolored. That means it is starting to oxidize. If this happens, clean out the dish completely, and make a new mixture of lavender water.

Can bronze clay be extruded?

Yes, bronze clay can be extruded through a plastic syringe. First condition the clay so it's workable. Add some lavender water to the clay to make it thin enough to be extruded. Place the clay in the syringe, but try to avoid trapping air bubbles. The clay is dense so it'll take a substantial amount of pressure to extrude it from the syringe. If you start suffering from hand fatigue, there's a tool available that makes it easier to press the clay out. It looks and acts like a mini caulk gun except, instead of caulk, you insert a syringe of metal clay.

EASY EXTRUDER

You can easily make a quick homemade piping bag. To do so, knead some lavender water into your clay. The consistency should be thinner than the lump clay, but thicker than slip. Place the clay in a plastic bag, and press it all into one corner. Cut a small hole in the corner of the bag, then twist the bag and apply pressure. The clay will squeeze out of the bag the same way icing is pressed out of a piping bag.

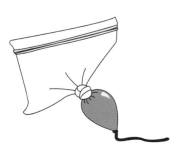

Bag Extruder

How do I join bronze clay pieces?

Pieces of bronze clay can be joined together several different ways. If attaching layers of moist clay together, a small amount of water can be brushed onto the surfaces of the clay. Gently press the pieces together to form a tight bond. This works best for pieces that have a wide surface area.

Slip is most often used to attach bronze clay pieces to one another. I usually mix slip on the fly—making just enough to use for the day. Take a thumbnail-sized lump of clay and pinch off small pieces. The smaller the pieces, the easier it will be to mix the slip. Place the pieces in a small jar or dish that can be easily covered. Use a spray bottle containing lavender water to mist the pieces of clay until the surfaces have a wet sheen. Cover the jar and allow the water to soak in. After a few minutes, the clay lumps should look soft. Using a pallet knife or a blending tool, mix the clay and water together until you get a thick yogurt-like consistency.

Slip Texture

To test for the correct texture, touch a blending tool to the surface of the slip, and pull up quickly. The slip should pull up into a soft peak. If it doesn't, it's probably too thick, so add more water. If the slip peaks but then falls back, too much water has been added. Add a couple more pinches of clay, and mix the slip together with a pallet knife. It's important not to add too much water, because if the slip is watery, it won't be very strong, which can lead to weak or broken joints in the fired piece.

It's super easy to use slip to attach two pieces of bronze clay. Using a blending tool, apply a good amount of slip to the area of clay where the join will be made. Press the second piece of clay into the slip so the two pieces are glued together. Some of the slip may squish out of the sides. If that happens, use a blending tool or paintbrush to blend the excess slip into the joint. Allow the slip to dry completely. Once it's dry, inspect the joint. Fill in any gaps or holes with more slip.

For really challenging joints, clay can be used. I use this method when joining two pieces of dried clay. Using clay this way is like the mortar between bricks: the wet clay will hold the two

TIM McCREIGHT
Untitled, 2008
5 x 5 x 0.5 cm
Bronze clay
Photo by artist

MARCO FLESERI
Atlantis Imperial Cuff No. 5, 2008
1 to 1.5 cm in width
Bronze clay
Photo by artist

15

pieces together tightly. To start, press a small lump of clay onto one of the dried pieces where the attachment is to be made. Brush a small amount of water on the lump to moisten it, but be careful not to overwet it. Press the second piece of dry clay onto the moistened clay lump, and then use a blending tool to blend in the clay around the edges. Allow the clay to dry completely. Once it's dry, inspect the seam for any gaps. If you find one, fill it in with a small piece of fresh clay. After the piece is completely dry, gently sand the joint with a nail file or fine sandpaper (I use 400 grit) to smooth it.

Bronze clay is so affordable; I'd like to use it to create larger pieces. What kinds of burnable cores can I use?

An armature (or core) is an internal support system that you cover with clay in order to build a structure. Armatures allow you to use less clay, resulting in a lighter weight piece, and are used when a form needs to be hollow. Any burnable form can be used with bronze clay. Cork, wood, and paper clay all work well, especially since you can sculpt them to the exact size and shape armature that's needed for your art pieces. After shaping your form, sculpt layers of clay over it and then let it dry. If your piece doesn't have a natural opening such as a hollow sculpture, you must incorporate one that's $1/8$ inch (3 mm) or larger into your design. Place the opening in an inconspicuous area so it doesn't interrupt the design flow. After the piece has been fired, the core can be removed and the hole patched with bronze clay, then refired. Firing bronze clay with a burnable form is slightly different from the regular firing schedules (see page 23).

I have some areas that need refining. At what stage should I do that?

With a steady hand and some focus, bronze clay can be refined while it's wet. I love refining the shape during this stage since it's one of the easiest ways to remove clay from your design. Once the basic shape has been formed, let the clay dry before doing any further refinement.

Leather-hard is a great in-between stage when the clay is mostly—but not completely—dry. If you need to make soft curves or bends in your piece, do it at this stage.

When working on finer details, it's easiest to refine the clay after it's bone dry. This allows you to handle the piece without distorting the texture and design. Most beauty supply shops carry a huge stock of files in different grits. Use a coarse file to reshape a piece or remove a large area. Follow the coarse file with a finer grit, removing any file marks left by the coarser file. After using the nail files, follow up with fine-grit sandpaper to remove any last file marks.

Even bone dry, bronze clay is still slightly pliable, making it prime for carving. Carving into the clay allows you to add texture, as well as refine and emphasize the texture that's already on the piece. The clay's pliability allows the tools to grab onto the clay and carve crisp fine lines. I like using linoleum and wood carvers for carving custom designs into the surface of the clay. Wax carvers and dental tools are great for getting into small spaces. Using carving tools can take some practice. If you're new to carving, take some time to experiment. It's well worth the effort to become familiar with your tools.

Once fired, the bronze is incredibly tough and will take a lot of elbow grease to file, so it's best to do as much filing and refining as you can before you fire your pieces. Do your filing over a piece of paper on your work surface. The filings that land on the paper can be saved to make slip or used as texture. If the clay you're filing catches or drags against the file, that means it's still damp. If this happens, set the piece aside and allow it to dry some more.

Does bronze clay need to be dry before firing?

Yes, it's best if the clay is as dry as possible before firing. By drying the clay first, you have the opportunity to refine any rough edges. Drying also reduces excess moisture in the clay that can steam and push out through your piece during firing, possibly causing damage. This can also leave bumps and bubbles on the surface of the clay, which isn't very pretty. A very small amount of moisture is okay, though, since it'll dry up before it gets hot enough to turn into steam.

To dry bronze clay you have several options. The easiest way to dry clay is simply to let it sit out and dry naturally. Air-drying is also the gentlest, allowing the clay to dry uniformly. If I have a large or thick piece, that's normally the method I choose. Of course, humidity can have an effect on how quickly your clay will dry. If you're working with clay on a humid day, it'll take longer.

To hasten drying, the clay can be dried with very low heat from a food dehydrator, warming tray (such as a coffee or tea warmer), or anything else that produces an even, low heat. If bronze clay is dried too quickly or if the dryer is too hot, it can crack or warp. This is because the surface of the clay dries very quickly while the inner clay is still wet. As the outer clay dries, it shrinks slightly. Dehydrators and warmers usually work well to dry the clay quickly with little warping or cracking.

My piece warped a little while drying. Is there anything I can do to fix it?

It's not a problem if the clay warps during drying. If you notice it warping, flip the piece over and apply gentle pressure to flatten it.

After drying, the clay is still slightly elastic, so there are a couple of ways to straighten a completely dry piece. The first is to hold it gently with your fingers and apply slight pressure to make the piece flat again. If the piece is stubborn, place it in the refrigerator for a few minutes. Cooling the dried clay helps it to relax. Once it's cool, gently press it into shape. Whether you're flattening the piece at room temperature or after you've cooled it, be sure to handle the piece gingerly.

And if all else fails, fire the piece as is. After firing, place the bronze on a bench block or anvil and use a rawhide mallet to flatten it.

CELIE FAGO
Untitled, 2008
6.8 x 7.5 cm each
Bronze clay; carved, heat patina
Photo by Douglas Foulke

JEANETTE LANDENWITCH
Wheelthrown Bowl, 2008
1.9 x 3.2 cm
Bronze clay
Photo by artist

Now that my piece is dry, I see some cracks. What should I do?

Cracks are accentuated during the firing process, so carefully inspect all the seams and joints on your pieces. If a crack is a fine hairline one, it can be filled in. Dip a paintbrush into water, and wipe away any excess. You want the brush to be wet, but not too wet. With a light touch, brush the cracked surface of the clay. The water will help knit the crack together.

Fine cracks can also be burnished together. Rub the flat side of a burnisher against the surface of the clay where the cracks are. The burnishing action will force the clay together, sealing the cracks.

If the crack is slightly larger than a hairline, you can use thick slip to repair it. With a rubber blending tool or a paintbrush, pick up a dollop of slip and apply it to the crack. Work the slip down into the crack with the blending tool. The slip will shrink slightly as it dries. If the crack is deep, the slip may shrink into the crack as it dries. If this happens, apply a second layer of slip to the crack and let it dry completely. Sand the slip to smooth, if necessary.

Medium to large cracks can be filled with clay. Wet the inside edges of the crack with a damp paintbrush. Tear off a small lump of fresh clay, and roll it into a thin snake that's about the same size as the crack. Press it into the moistened area, and then blend and smooth the clay with a rubber-tipped blending tool. Let the clay dry completely, and sand the surface to smooth it.

Can I fire stones in place with bronze clay?

Yes, most synthetic stones that can be fired with silver metal clay can be fired in place with bronze clay. I've found that white cubic zirconia, laboratory-grown corundum (rubies and sapphires), and laboratory-grown spinel are all safe options. When shopping for lab-grown stones, stay away from anything that is described as a doublet or triplet. These types of stones are actually several layers of stone glued together with a colored epoxy. The glue doesn't survive the firing temperatures needed to fire bronze clay, so the stones will lose all their color and look burnt or cloudy after firing. The two natural stones I've had good luck firing in place are peridot and garnet.

The firing temperature for bronze clay is too high to fire any glass in place. Most glass will become soft and begin to flow during the firing. Lots of different mosaic tiles and china can withstand

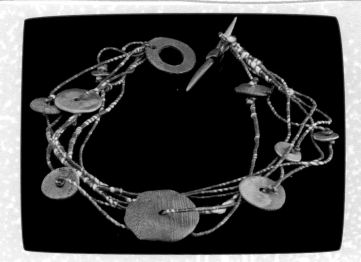

PATRIK KUSEK
Discs Bracelet, 2008
14 x 4 cm
Bronze clay, silk; heat patina
Photo by artist

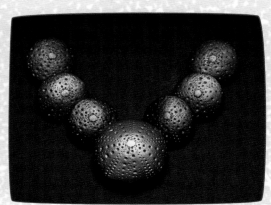

BILL STRUVE
Sea Urchin Necklace, 2008
17 x 13 x 1 cm
Bronze clay, lentil beads
Photo by Laurence Maultsby

the temperatures, but there are some glazes that may not survive. To test whether a tile will work, fire a small sample piece in a kiln at 1550°F (843°C) for half an hour. Allow the kiln to cool before taking the piece out. If the surface bubbled or changed colors, then it can't be embedded. If the surface looks like it did before firing, it can be fired with the clay. This is the type of test that was done with the tiles used for the Mosaic Bracelet (page 34).

When embedding a stone or tile into bronze clay, you need to make sure that it's buried into the clay so that it's captured in place as the clay shrinks around it. If the stone is sitting too high in the clay, it'll be forced up and out as the clay shrinks.

What types of findings can be fired in place?

Any finding or wire that is made out of bronze, copper, or brass can be fired in place. Because the metals are very similar, they will fuse together during firing. There are manufactured findings available, or you can make them yourself using wire or sheet.

Silver findings won't fuse into place, since bronze and silver metals are too dissimilar. You'll need to capture silver findings like you do gemstones.

Can I fire bronze clay and silver clay together?

Firing bronze clay and silver clay together while they're both raw doesn't work, since the bronze clay must be fired in activated carbon. Silver clay doesn't sinter (the fusing point where a metal is able to bond to itself) when fired in activated carbon. The binder in the clay burns away, but the silver particles don't sinter together. This leaves the silver with a fragile, chalky feel that breaks easily.

The way to work around this dilemma is to first fire the silver clay according to the manufacturer's directions. The fired silver piece can then be embedded into raw bronze clay. The key here is to embed the silver so the bronze clay surrounds it. Fine silver and bronze won't fuse together. Because of the 17 to 20 percent shrinkage that occurs when bronze clay is fired, the embedded silver will become locked into place.

PATRIK KUSEK
Lotus Bowl, 2008
6 x 6 cm
Bronze clay; torn
Textures courtesy of Celie Fago
Photo by artist

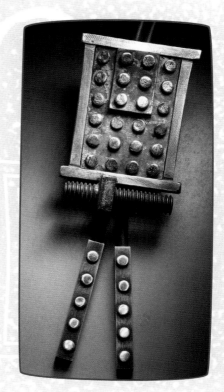

MARK NELSON
With These, We Built Our Empires, 2008
65 x 40 x 10 cm
Bronze clay from mold, sterling silver, steel, rubber
Photo by Tara Anderson

HADAR JACOBSON
Two Pods, 2008
7 x 3 x 3 cm
Bronze clay, silver clay; fired
Photo by artist

GAIL LANNUM
Annia's Shield, 2008
2.5 x 2.8 cm
Bronze clay
Photo by artist

Can I use a torch, hot pot, or the stovetop to fire bronze clay?

Because bronze clay has such a long firing time, and because it needs to be contained in activated carbon, it can only be fired in a kiln. Torches, hot pots, and stovetop firing won't work for a couple of different reasons. First, they don't produce enough consistent heat to fire the clay. Also, the clay needs to be fired for several hours; six to nine hours is the average firing time for bronze clay pieces. Hot pots and stovetops typically can't handle this length of time—and who wants to hold a torch for six to nine hours anyway? So for firing, bronze clay has to be in an enclosed kiln.

How do I prepare my bronze clay piece for firing?

Once the clay has been formed, dried, and refined, it's time to fire it. Besides a kiln, there are three things that are an absolute must for the bronze clay firing process—a container to fire in, activated carbon, and a dust mask.

Firing Containers

The first thing you need is a stainless-steel container that'll hold your piece during firing. This container must be heat-tolerant and needs to fit comfortably into the kiln. Bain-Marie containers (the kind used to hold and heat foods in a buffet line) are a perfect choice to use as a firing container. They come in a variety of sizes and shapes, so you're sure to find one that fits your kiln. Other containers such as steel beakers or alumina crucibles can also be used. I recommend using ceramic feet or risers on the floor of the

Firing Container

kiln to support the firing container. This will keep the container off the floor, allowing for even heat to surround the container during firing.

CONTAIN YOURSELF

Feeling industrious—or just thrifty? You can even build your own firing container using steel foil. The edges of the foil are super sharp, so make sure you use heavy-duty work gloves when working with it. Fold the foil into any size pouch, envelope, or box that you need. A steel foil pouch is a great option when you only have a few small pieces to fire, as you don't need much activated carbon. Also, when firing, the pouch will heat up faster than a larger container. Steel foil tool wrap can be purchased at online industrial suppliers.

Another way you can make a container is with three square-shaped soldering pads. Using a saw, cut one pad into four equal-sized pieces. These pieces will form the walls of your container. Nail the sawn pieces to one of the full soldering pads. Fill the container with activated carbon and your bronze clay piece. Use the third pad as a lid. Note: the nails will oxidize during the firing process, but this won't interfere with the way the bronze fires.

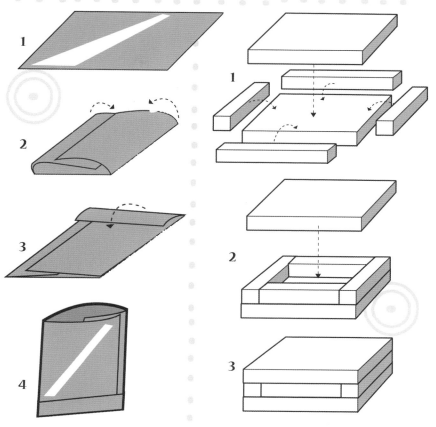

I prefer using a container that has a lid. This helps prevent too much of the carbon from burning away during firing. A lid also helps keep your kiln clean. No matter what, there will be soot in the kiln after firing. But if you use a lid, you can keep the soot to a minimum.

Most suppliers who carry bronze clay will have firing containers available. You can also find them at restaurant supply stores.

Activated Carbon

Once you have your container, you need activated carbon, which is different from regular carbon or charcoal. When carbon is "activated," it's put through a process that makes the carbon particles extremely porous. Under magnification, the pieces of carbon look like small sea sponges.

Now it's time for a quick science lesson. The carbon is used to absorb the oxygen that's present in the kiln during firing, creating a mostly oxygen-free atmosphere. Oxygen is attracted to copper, especially when the copper is heated. And since bronze clay is 89 percent copper, oxygen really loves it. When copper is heated, oxygen attaches itself to the copper, creating copper oxide. This oxide prevents the copper and tin particles from sintering together. That's why you need activated carbon. The activated carbon has a lot of surface area to absorb the oxygen before it can attach itself to the bronze. So it acts as a barrier, allowing the bronze to fully sinter.

There are two types of activated carbon that are commonly used with bronze clay. The first is made from coconut shell. This carbon completely protects the clay and leaves very little surface color on the bronze after firing. When the clay is fired in coconut shell carbon, the fired bronze comes out of the kiln looking like raw, unpolished bronze. At times, the surface of the bronze may show some color variations, usually in the light to dark brown range.

The second type of activated carbon is coal based and has been acid-washed. This carbon will leave a kiln patina on the surface of the bronze. These beautiful rainbow colors are completely random and aren't controllable. They can range from muted browns and greens to vibrant blues, purples, and pinks. The finish can be preserved with wax or lacquer, although the colors will become darker. If left unpolished, the colors will eventually rub away, revealing the natural color of the bronze.

The first time it's used, activated carbon should be prefired. This prefiring will burn away any organic material that may be in the carbon. To prefire, fill the firing container full of activated carbon. Place it in the kiln and fire at a full ramp to 1550°F (843°C). Hold the temperature for half an hour. Let the container cool to room temperature before removing it from the kiln. The carbon is now ready to fire with bronze clay.

Over time the carbon will be less effective. If you notice that your fired pieces are fragile or prone to breaking, this could be because the carbon is spent. The carbon will start to break down somewhere between 100–150 hours of firing. Dispose of the carbon and refire your pieces in fresh prefired carbon.

Dust Mask

No matter what kind of activated carbon you choose, always wear a dust mask when working with it. Although the carbon is in granular form, it can be very dusty, especially when it's been used, and can be harmful if inhaled. So be sure to wear a dust mask any time you're loading or unloading the kiln.

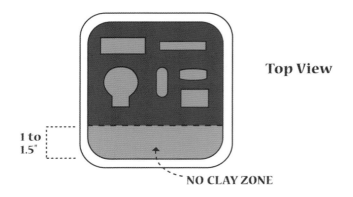

Top View

1 to 1.5"

NO CLAY ZONE

FIRING CONTAINER

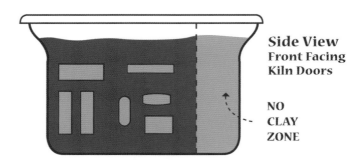

Side View
Front Facing Kiln Doors

NO CLAY ZONE

Loading the Firing Container

It's important to make sure the bronze is completely surrounded by activated carbon before firing. Fill your firing container so it has 1/2 to 1 inch (1.3 to 2.5 cm) of carbon on the bottom. Place your bronze clay piece on the carbon. If you're firing more than one piece, leave about 1/2 inch (1.3 cm) between them. Take care that the clay doesn't touch the walls of the firing container. Add another layer of activated carbon on top of the bronze pieces. At this point, additional layers of bronze clay can be added—kind of like building a bronze clay lasagna. Once all your layers are in place, top off the container with a final layer of activated carbon. Place the lid on the container and put it into the kiln.

If you're using a front-loading kiln, keep in mind that the temperature near the door can be slightly lower than what the kiln readout is saying. This may keep the pieces in the firing container from sintering completely. I find it's best to just avoid placing any pieces toward the front of the container that will be closest to the door. Consider the front 1 to 1½ inches (2.5 to 3.8 cm) of the container a "no clay zone." This will ensure that all the pieces being fired are completely sintered.

If you're firing several pieces at once, make note of how many pieces are placed in the firing container. Once all the pieces are tucked into the carbon, it's impossible to see them. So to make it easier on you to remember, jot down how many pieces are in the container. To make it foolproof, use your digital camera to take a picture of each layer before it's covered with carbon. This will give you a map of exactly what pieces are in the firing and show exactly what position they were in inside the container. The photos will remind you how many pieces need to be fished out of the carbon, and if there was a firing problem with one of them, knowing its position in the kiln helps. This may help identify any cool spots that occur in the kiln during firing.

Firing Schedule

There are three parts to a bronze clay firing schedule: ramp, target temperature, and hold time. Ramp is how quickly or slowly the kiln heats up. Most kilns used for metal clay ramp by the hour. The second part of the schedule is the target temperature. This is the temperature that you want the kiln to hold at. And the final part of the schedule is the hold time, or the duration the kiln will maintain the target temperature.

There are two recommended firing schedules for bronze clay. The first—called the short firing schedule—is for thin pieces less than ⅛ inch (3 mm) thick. The second schedule, also know as the long firing schedule, can be used for thin pieces as well as pieces up to ⅜ inch (10 mm) thick. When you aren't sure which schedule to use, use the long firing schedule.

Short Firing Schedule
Ramp: 500°F (260°C) per hour
Target temperature: 1550°F (843°C)
Hold time: 2 hours

Long Firing Schedule
Ramp: 250°F (121°C) per hour
Target temperature: 1550°F (843°C)
Hold time: 3 hours

JEANETTE LANDENWITCH
Ye Olde Tree Trunk, 2008
13.3 x 6.4 cm
Bronze clay, silver metal clay
Photo by artist

HADAR JACOBSON
Scale, 2008
7 x 4 x 0.5 cm
Bronze clay, silver clay, copper, sapphires; fired
Photo by artist

23

If you are firing larger or thicker pieces, the ramp rate can be slowed down and the hold time can be set longer. For example, when firing the Coasters del Sol (page 60), I used a firing schedule with a 150°F (65°C) per hour ramp with a four-hour hold time. I did this to ensure that the heat soaks into the piece completely, allowing it to fully sinter.

What is the firing procedure if I'm using a form?

When buried in activated carbon, the form won't burn out completely. This results in two problems. First, the form will burn, but not burn away. This means that a lump of burned material is left inside the piece. If the piece has only a small opening, like a bead, it's very difficult to remove the burned material. But the bigger problem is that most of the time the clay won't sinter completely. This leaves you with a fragile piece that feels slightly spongy and is prone to breaking easily.

Once the clay is totally dry, the piece can be prefired in a kiln without any activated carbon. This prefiring is a short process that will burn away most of the form. This process, called open-air firing, was first suggested by Darnall Burks and tested extensively by Bill Struve and others.

To burn out the form, place the piece on a kiln shelf that's supported on posts. Ramp the kiln at 280°F (138°C) per hour and hold at 560°F (293°C) for 15 minutes. Allow the piece to cool so it can be handled easily. Gently remove any of the core that didn't burn out completely. At this stage, the piece can be slightly fragile. It's about the same strength as dried original silver clay. Place the prefired piece into a firing container with activated carbon, and fire as usual.

How long should I let my piece cool in the kiln?

It's best to let the firing container cool naturally. You can remove the container from the kiln while it's still hot, but it's best to keep the pieces in the carbon until they're cool, 300°F (149°C) or less. If you can comfortably handle the container with regular oven mitts, it's okay to empty it. If the bronze pieces are taken out of the carbon while they're still very hot, they'll oxidize as soon as they come in contact with the air. This will result in additional cleanup time.

You can also keep the container in the kiln until it's cool. To expedite the cooling process, open the door to the kiln once the firing has completed. This will "crash cool" the kiln, allowing the heat to escape quickly. Kilns with firebrick liners will retain the heat longer than kilns that have a fiber liner.

TERRY KOVALCIK
Meadow's Edge, **2008**
Largest, 3.5 x 1.7 x 0.7 cm
Bronze clay; carved, hollow
oval center, patina
Photo by Corrin Jacobsen Kovalcik

How do I clean my piece once I take it out of the carbon?

All you need to do is rinse it in water. Sometimes for highly textured pieces, the carbon may need to be picked out of any crevices.

My fired piece has a crack. Can it be fixed?

Sometimes after firing, cracks can appear in the clay. Although this can be disappointing, it's not a loss. Simply force some clay or slip into the crack, let the piece dry, and then sand away any excess clay to blend the seam. Refire the piece using the short firing schedule (ramp 500°F [260°C]/hour and hold at 1550°F [843°C] for two hours).

What types of finishes can be achieved with bronze clay?

You'll find that the bronze has a great finish straight out of the kiln. If you tumble your piece, you can achieve a high polish on the bronze. Using a buffing motor or flex shaft can garner all sorts of finish results—satin, high polish, or mirror.

When fired in coal-based carbon, you can get lots of fun, random colors. These colors can be sealed in place using lacquer or a sealing wax, but be aware that doing so will make the kiln colors become slightly darker.

When using coconut shell carbon, you get little to no color at all. If I plan on doing a special finish or adding my own colors after firing, I choose coconut carbon.

You can also get colors on the bronze after firing by using a torch. First finish the piece to the desired finish—high polish, matte finish, etc. Wash the piece well so that the surface is completely clean. Place the bronze piece on a soldering brick, and, using a torch with a soft, bushy flame, gently pass the flame across the surface of the bronze. Just a little bit of heat on the surface will give the bronze a rainbow of color.

To get a true bronze or gold color on your piece, polish the surface with a progression of fine sandpaper or polishing wheels. This will give a bright gold color to the bronze. I use 1200, 4000, 6000, and 8000 grits to produce a high shine on fired bronze.

ANNEALING

The bronze that comes out of the kiln is very strong and durable. It can be a challenge to drill into if you need to make a hole in it after firing. If you find the bronze doesn't drill easily, it can be annealed. Annealing is a process used to soften the metal using heat.

To anneal bronze, place the fired piece on a soldering block or in an annealing tray. In a dimly lit room, use a torch to heat the bronze to a dull red color. Hold at that color for a minute or so. Remove the heat, and let the bronze cool just enough so the redness goes away. Once the glow is gone, pick up the bronze with tweezers and quench it in water. The piece will now be covered in a black oxide layer. This layer can be removed by letting it soak in warm pickle for a few minutes.

Can patinas be used on bronze clay?

One of the most exciting things about working with bronze clay is all the colors you can achieve on its surface by using different oxidizers or patinas. There are a lot of commercially manufactured patinas available, but many of these are made with harsh chemicals. When using these types of patinas, make sure you're working in an area with plenty of ventilation. You can also use a homemade patina. I like using ammonia fuming or sawdust wet with ammonia. Both create beautiful green and blue colors, but the process can take anywhere from several hours to several days, depending on the color intensity you want.

To ammonia fume, you need one small plastic or glass container. Fill the bowl with about ¼ cup (60 mL) of ammonia, and place it in a larger container that has a lid with a tight seal. Wet the fired bronze piece with water so the surface is moist. Pack table salt onto the wet surface so it adheres. Place the salted bronze into the larger container next to the bowl of ammonia. Seal the container, trapping the ammonia fumes. Leave the lid on for a couple of days to let the fumes do their work. The salt on the surface will react with the ammonia fumes, leaving a fantastic green surface. This is pretty much how the Statue of Liberty got her color.

JEANETTE LANDENWITCH
Bezel-set Agate, **2008**
45.7 cm in length
Bronze clay pendant and beads, sterling silver
spacer beads, agate beads, agate cabochon
Photo by artist

MARIAELENA BACA
Pointing the Way, **2008**
20 cm in length
Bronze clay, brass wire, jasper
Photo by Tara Anderson

Ammonia Fuming

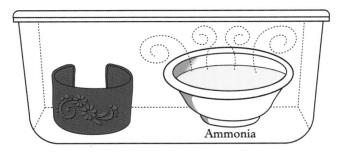

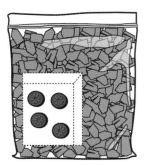

Closed Zipper Bag with Wood Chips

To get subtle mottled colors on the surface,
you'll need some cedar chips (the kind used for
lining pet cages) or sawdust—making sure the
sawdust is made of only wood and not particle
board, since you never know what kind of glue is
used in it. Place the chips or sawdust in a plastic
container with a lid or in a plastic zipper bag. Add
just enough ammonia to the chips or dust to wet it.
You don't want it to be soaked, but it should be well
saturated. Bury your bronze pieces in the mixture,
and let them sit for several hours or several days.
You can keep tabs on your progress by pulling
them out of the mixture to check the color. If it's
not what you want, just stick it back into the mix
and let it sit for another day or two.

Can bronze clay be soldered?

Yes, fired bronze clay can easily be soldered. Silver
solder is the simplest to use and is readily available
from most jewelry suppliers. It comes in several
forms—sheet, wire, chips, and paste. The drawback
to using silver solder is the color won't match the
bronze so don't use it on visible seams. Silver solder
also works great when soldering silver and bronze
together to get a two-toned piece.

BRONZE CLAY SOLDERING KIT
Have these items at hand for any soldering project in this book.

- *Torch*
- *Solder*
- *High heat block*
- *Charcoal soldering block*
- *Solder pick*
- *Flux*
- *Flux brush*
- *Fire coat (boric acid/denatured alcohol mixture)*
- *Soldering tweezers*
- *Pickle*
- *Pickle pot*
- *Copper tongs*

Because it comes in different hardnesses, silver solder is perfect when you need to solder multiple solder joints on your piece. Typically solder is available in hard, medium, and easy—each with a different melting point. For your first joint, you would use hard solder since it takes the most heat to melt. For your second joint, use medium solder. Since medium solder melts at a lower temperature than hard solder, you can create enough heat to make the medium solder flow while not interrupting the previous hard solder joint.

Copper solder is another good choice. It's not a true color match, but it's pretty darn close to the color of bronze. I use copper solder if my joint will be visible. Most often, copper solder is sold in wire form and comes in only one type of hardness.

There are yellow-colored solders that more closely match the bronze in color, but I find them difficult to use in comparison to silver or copper solder. The flow point has a wide variance so it's harder to control while soldering.

The last alternative is gold solder. The color matches beautifully but as you might expect, it's much more expensive than any other type of solder.

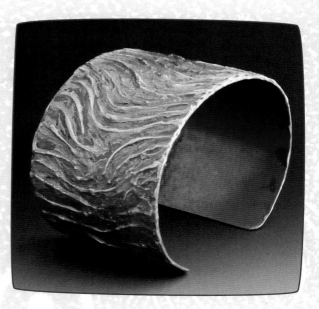

MARCO FLESERI
Untitled Cuff, 2008
5 cm in width
Bronze clay, copper
Photo by artist

DAWN WILSON-ENOCH
Desert Bangles, Sunring, and
Down the Arroyo, 2008–2009
Largest, 10.5 cm wide
Bronze clay, polymer with sand; patina, fired, hand finished
Photo by Margot Geist

MARCO FLESERI
The God of Past Loves Pendant, 2008
2 x 2 x 7.5 cm
Bronze clay
Photo by artist

DAWN WILSON-ENOCH
Cactus Remnants, 2009
Largest, 9 cm
Bronze clay; molded from cactus forms,
patina, fired, hand finished
Photo by Margot Geist

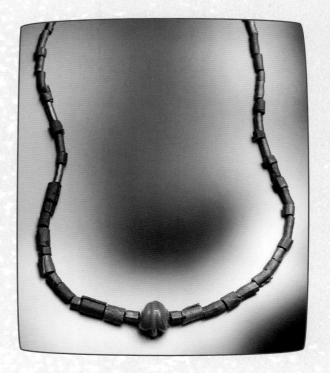

TERRY KOVALCIK
Thorny Vine Ankle Bracelet, 2008
23.7 cm in length
Bronze clay, liver of sulphur; sculpted, patina
Photo by Corrin Jacobsen Kovalcik

SESSIN DURGHAM
Garbanzo Beads, 2008
60.9 cm
Bronze clay, beads; hand rolled,
extruded, flameworked
Photo by Tara Anderson

PATRIK KUSEK
Ring & Shake Bracelet, 2008
10 x 10 mm
Bronze clay; torn, carved
Photo by artist

BARBARA BECKER SIMON
Benin Bangle, 2008
0.4 x 10 cm
Bronze clay; carved
Photo by Larry Sanders

HOLLACE ANN STRUVE
Woodland Fairy (Leaf), 2008
33 x 26 x 25 cm
Bronze clay
Photo by Laurence Maultsby

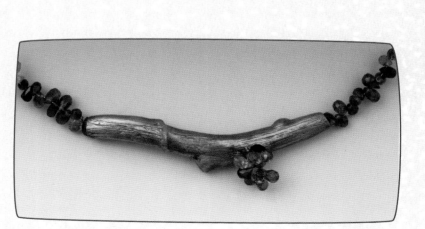

NISA SMILEY
Bronze Samara Earrings, 2008
5.7 x 1.9 cm
Bronze clay; soldered, patina, fired, forged
Photo by Robert Diamante

HADAR JACOBSON
Branch, 2008
5 x 0.5 x 0.5 cm
Bronze clay, garnets; fired
Photo by artist

BRONZE
METAL CLAY

TROUBLESHOOTING

Some say one of the best ways to learn is through our mistakes. And, boy, have I made my share! As with any new medium, there's lots of trial and error. Here are a few common problems—and fixes—that I encountered when first working with bronze clay.

BEFORE FIRING

Problem	What Happened	What You Can Do About It
As you're working with bronze clay it becomes stiff, even though it's still moist.	Bronze clay works best when it's cool. As it's being worked, body heat from your hands transfers into the clay.	If your clay becomes stiff, wrap it in plastic wrap. Place the wrapped clay in the refrigerator for a few minutes to allow the clay to cool down.
Cracks form on the surface of the clay as it's being worked.	The clay needed more hydration.	Use a spray bottle of water to spray the clay as it's being worked. It also helps to use a fair amount of pressure when rolling or kneading the clay, as this helps to seal any cracks that may occur while working.
After you roll out the clay, it looks like there are bubbles just under the surface.	These bubbles are small pockets of trapped air.	When these bubbles occur, poke the surface of the clay with a needle tool and then continue rolling the clay out. This will allow the air to escape from inside the clay.
Your hands and nails look green after working with bronze clay.	This is a result of handling copper for an extended amount of time—remember that bronze clay is 89% copper.	The best way to prevent this is to wipe away any clay or dust that can build up on your hands as you're working with it. I typically keep a shop rag at my bench so I can wipe off my hands as I'm working. After sanding bronze clay, you may find that some of the filings end up under your nails, leaving them a funky green shade. Usually some good hand soap and a nailbrush is enough to clean them. If you find the skin under your nails is stained, place a small amount of cuticle cream under your nail, then use a cuticle stick to clean away the cream. Another way to avoid this staining is to wear tight-fitting rubber gloves when working with bronze clay.

AFTER FIRING

Problem	What Happened	What You Can Do About It
 **Bubbles on the surface**	Bubbles on the surface of the fired bronze can be caused by a couple of things. The first is the clay wasn't completely dry before it was put into the kiln. The moisture in the clay turned to steam during firing and pushed the surface of the clay out as it escaped. The other reason for bubbles is there was air trapped in the clay as it was being formed. The trapped air will expand as it's being heated, causing the surface to bubble. See the previous page to learn how to prevent bubbles from forming.	Most small bubbles can be fixed after firing by using a small hammer to tap them into place. To do this, place the fired bronze on a bench block or anvil. Use a hammer with a rounded head, such as a chasing hammer, to tap the bubble down.
 **Cracks**	Cracks will form on the surface if there is a small crack in the unfired clay. These cracks are a result of the clay shrinking. As it shrinks, the clay is moving, finding the path of least resistance. If there is a small crack to begin with, there will be a larger crack after firing.	To repair cracks, fill in the gaps with clay or slip and refire. To prevent cracks from happening, make sure the clay is well conditioned, and use pressure as it's being kneaded.
Layers that were attached together with slip fell apart	If the slip is too thin, it will make a weak attachment. This is because there's too much water in the slip. The excess moisture waters down the clay, separating the copper and tin particles, thus preventing them from forming a solid joint.	When making slip, use the smallest amount of water possible. The slip needs to be thick like yogurt or pudding. It's also a good idea to stir the slip occasionally as you're using it. The pieces can be attached again and refired. Place a good amount of thick slip on the area that needs to be repaired. Reattach the embellishment by pressing it into the slip. Once the slip is dry, the item can be fired again using the short firing schedule.

AFTER FIRING

Problem	What Happened	What You Can Do About It
Pieces break or crumble	Typically, broken or crumbled pieces have been under-fired. This is due to the schedule the piece was fired at, or the way the piece was positioned in the firing container.	When firing thick pieces, it's best to follow the long firing schedule. This will ensure the heat penetrates the firing container, the carbon, and the clay enough to sinter the clay completely. Pieces placed in the center of the firing container receive less heat than those placed around the back and sides of the container. So, it's best to place thicker or larger items about $1/2$ inch (1.3 cm) from the inside edge of the firing container. When loading the firing container into a front-loading kiln, it's best to avoid the front of the container that will be closest to the door. The first inch (2.5 cm) or so closest to the door is cooler than the rest of the kiln. Because of this heat discrepancy, the bronze clay won't fully fire.
  Large piece sounds hollow after firing	Very large pieces that are over $3/4$ inch (1.9 cm) thick won't sinter all the way through. This is typical of any thick piece made of bronze clay. The hollow sound is the unfired bronze clay in the center of the piece. This usually isn't a problem, since the outside shell of the clay is fired solid.	Make sure the piece is fired through as completely as possible by using the long firing schedule. This schedule takes a while to complete, but it's worth it to have a fully sintered piece. If possible, drill a small hole in an inconspicuous place on the item being fired. This hole will give another direction for the clay to sinter. A good example of this is the hole drilled in the center of the Incense Vessel (page 114). The hole in the middle of the incense holder allowed the thick bottom piece of the vessel to fire all the way through.

Problem	What Happened	What You Can Do About It

You fired your bronze clay in the coal-based carbon, and there wasn't any color on the surface.

Coal is a funny thing. Since coal comes from so many sources, it's difficult to get carbon that is consistent. The color all depends on where the coal was mined, what minerals were also present in the mine, and how the coal was processed.

There's not a whole lot you can do. Since there are so many variables, it's difficult to say which batch of coal will leave color on the surface of the fired bronze. But that's half the fun of firing in the coal-based activated carbon. Sometimes the bronze comes out with really cool intense colors, and other times there isn't much color at all.

Your bronze turned pink when you pickled it after soldering.

Pickle chemical is a mild acid that removes any firescale from the surface of the bronze. Firescale is the black stuff that forms when the copper in the bronze is heated to high temperatures. The pickling process, while removing the firescale, leaves a thin layer of copper on the surface, which is why it looks pink.

To remove this layer, lightly brush the surface of the bronze with a soft steel brush or a coarse fiber sanding pad.

JEANETTE LANDENWITCH
In the Jungle, 2008
43.2 cm in length
Bronze clay, gold-filled spacer beads, turquoise beads
Photo by artist

MOSAIC BRACELET

Mosaic tiles tolerate the firing temperatures of bronze clay, come in a rainbow of colors, and bring a whole new look to jewelry designs.

NEEDED

- Bronze clay tool kit, page 12
- 5 mosaic tiles, each ⅜ inch (1 cm) square
- Six craft sticks
- Craft glue
- ⅜-inch-square (1 cm) cutter
- Large drinking straw or round pen barrel
- Bronze clay slip
- Chain-nose pliers
- Toggle or other clasp with jump ring, commercial or handmade

HERE'S HOW

1. To determine the height of your risers, measure the thickness of the mosaic tiles, and add 2 mm to this measurement. (My tiles were 4 mm thick, therefore, my risers for this project were 6 mm tall.) To make the risers, stack craft sticks together until they reach the required height. Use craft glue to adhere the stacked craft sticks together. Once you have assembled two risers, set the pair aside to dry.

2. Place a lump of bronze clay on your work surface, and position the risers on either side of the clay. Roll the clay into a slab. With the tissue blade, cut a ¾-inch (1.9 cm) square from the slab. Center the ⅜-inch-square (1 cm) clay cutter on the slab. Press the cutter through the clay to cut a square hole in the center.

3. Position a mosaic tile over the cutout square. Gently press the tile through the opening, and embed it approximately 1 mm below the surface of the clay. Allow the clay to dry completely. Repeat steps 2 and 3 to make five pieces total.

4. Smooth all sides of the dried clay squares, including the tops and bottoms, with the emery file. Keep the file from coming into contact with the mosaic tiles to avoid scratching.

5. To make the loops that attach to the tile pieces, first rub a thin layer of oil on the drinking straw or round pen barrel. On your work surface, roll a fresh lump of clay into a thin snake. Gently lift the snake, and wrap it around the drinking straw to form a coil of five rings (figure 1). If the snake is not long enough, roll a second one and wrap it onto the straw next to the previous snake. Allow the coil to dry on the straw.

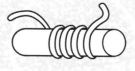

figure 1

6. Remove the dry coil from the straw. Using a craft knife, cut the rings of the coil apart. Cut each ring in half, forming two semicircles. Use the emery file to sand the ends of each semicircle flat.

7. With the paintbrush, apply water to one of the outside edges of one tile piece. Apply slip to the ends of one semicircle with the blending tool. Center the semicircle on the outside edge of the square, and press the ends into place. Use the blending tool to blend in any excess slip, and let dry. Repeat this step to adhere another semicircle on the opposite side of the tile.

8. Check for gaps where the semicircles meet the tile. Fill in any gaps with slip, and let dry. Lightly sand the rings if necessary. Repeat steps 7 and 8 for the remaining tile pieces.

9. To make the jump rings that connect the tiles, first rub a thin layer of oil on the large drinking straw or round pen barrel. On your work surface, roll a fresh lump of clay into a long, thin snake. Gently lift the snake, and wrap it around the large straw or pen barrel to form a coil. Allow the coil to dry completely, and then use the craft knife to cut the coil into five rings.

10. Gently flex open one ring and attach it to the loops of two tile pieces (figure 2). Position the ends of the ring together. Wet the ends of the ring with a paintbrush. Roll a very small ball of clay with your fingertips. Press the ball into the seam of the ring. Use the blending tool to smooth the clay into place. Allow the ring to dry. Repeat this step to connect the remaining tile pieces.

figure 2

11. Gently sand the outside edges of the rings with the emery file. File the inside edges of the rings with the round needle file.

12. Place the bracelet in the activated coconut carbon, and arrange it so the rings and tile pieces have as little contact with each other as possible. Using the long firing schedule, fire the bracelet in the kiln.

13. Rinse the fired bracelet in water. If any rings are stuck together, gently pry them apart with your hands. Run the fiber pad over the entire surface of the bracelet, being careful not to sand the surface of the tiles, to give it a matte finish. Use the chain-nose pliers to open the jump ring on the clasp. Attach the clasp to one end of the bracelet.

ANCIENT TREASURES

The repetitive, symmetrical design of this pendant suggests a sacred mandala. Mandalas are used to connect one to the universe through contemplation.

Bronze clay kit, page 12

Circle template, 1½ inch
   (3.8 cm) in diameter

Bronze slip

Carving tool

Drinking straw

Photocopied bail template,
   page 122

Bronze oxidizer

Steel brush

Necklace cord or chain of
   your choice

1. Place the bronze clay on your work surface, and roll a slab that is four cards thick. Use the circle template (figure 1) and a craft knife to cut a circle of clay that is 1½ inches (3.8 cm) in diameter. Let the clay circle dry, and then smooth its edge with the emery file.

2. Use the markings on the circle template to draw lines on the dried clay circle, dividing it into eight equal sections (figure 1). (The circle should look like a pie with eight identical pieces.) These markings will help to keep the design centered on the circle.

3. Roll a small ball of bronze clay, and attach it to the center of the circle with slip. Press the tip of the blending tool into the center of the ball to make a dimple.

4. Roll a slab of bronze clay that is three cards thick. Use the craft knife to cut four narrow diamond shapes, each ½ inch (1.3 cm) long. Apply some slip along the pencil line that is in the 12-o'clock position. Place the diamond shape on the slip, making sure the bottom point of the diamond touches the center ball. Press the diamond into place with your fingertip. Wick water around the edge of the diamond to create a bond. Repeat this process with the three remaining diamonds at the three-, six-, and nine-o'clock positions.

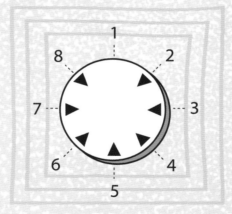

figure 1

5. Roll a slab of bronze clay that is three cards thick. Cut seven very small triangles, each approximately ⅛ inch (3 mm) long. Except at the 12-o'clock position, use slip to attach a small triangle to the edge of the circle on the markings made earlier (figure 2). (The bail will be placed later on the 12-o'clock mark.)

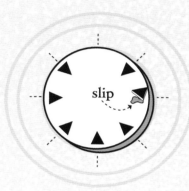

slip

figure 2

6. Roll a slab of bronze clay that is three cards thick. Cut four very small diamond shapes. Use slip to attach a small clay diamond between each of the long clay diamonds, and press into place. For added dimension, roll small amounts of clay into eight balls with your fingertips. Symmetrically place the balls in each quadrant, attaching them with slip. Let the pendant dry completely.

7. Using the carving tool, create decorative lines on the edge of the pendant as well as on top of the diamonds, triangles, and balls.

8. To create the bail, first oil the drinking straw. Roll out a three-cards-thick slab of bronze clay that is fresh out of the package. Use the photocopied bail template and a craft knife to cut out the bail. Drape the cut clay around the drinking straw (figure 3). Allow the bail to dry completely.

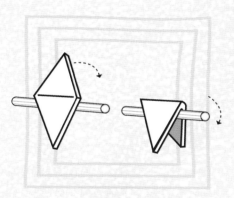

figure 3

9. Gently sand the edges of the dry bail with the emery file. Place some thick slip on the front and back of the pendant at the 12-o'clock position. Straddle the bail over the top of the pendant, matching the tips of the bail to the slip. Press the bail into the slip and hold it in place until the slip is dry. Use the blending tool to smooth away any excess slip.

10. Place the pendant in the activated coconut carbon, and fire it in the kiln using the short firing schedule.

11. Following the manufacturer's instructions, use a black oxidizer to create a patina on the fired pendant. Use a steel brush to remove the oxidation from the surface of the pendant and to give it a satin finish. String the pendant on the necklace cord or chain of your choice.

CORONA PENDANT

Circles and triangles—two straightforward shapes—yet in this project they unite to form an intricate pendant with an ancient feel.

Bronze clay tool kit, page 12

Circle cutter, ⁵⁄₈ inch (1.6 cm) in diameter

Triangle needle file

Half-round needle file

Drinking straw

Leather cord

20-gauge jump ring, 5 mm

Bronze oxidizer

Making the Pendant

1. Place the bronze clay on your work surface, and roll a slab that is three cards thick. Using the ⁵⁄₈-inch (1.6 cm) circle cutter, cut nine circles of clay. Place the circles under plastic wrap to keep them moist.

2. Using the craft knife, cut eight metal clay triangles, each ¹⁄₈ inch (3 mm) long. Cut one additional triangle that is ¹⁄₂ inch (1.3 cm) long. Place all of the clay triangles under the plastic wrap with the circles.

3. Roll another slab of bronze clay two cards thick. This slab should measure approximately 3 x 4¹⁄₂ inches (7.6 x 11.4 cm) to support the circle and triangle pieces. Wet the surface of the clay with the paintbrush.

4. Begin building the pendant by placing one circle in the center of the slab, about ¹⁄₄ inch (6 mm) inside the top edge. Pat down the circle to make sure it sticks to the slab. If necessary, wet around the edge of the circle to make certain it sticks. Nestle two more circles under and on either side of the first circle, making sure the edges are touching. Pat down the circles to make them stick. Continue the "place and pat" method, positioning three circles on the third row, two circles on the fourth row, and one circle on the last row.

5. Wet the entire surface of the clay with the paintbrush to keep it moist. Place the large clay triangle underneath the bottom circle. Place the smaller triangles, points out, around the perimeter of the pendant and nestled between each circle. Use the wet paintbrush to add more water as necessary to make the triangles stick to the surface.

6. Use the craft knife to cut a ¹⁄₄-inch (6 mm) semicircle above the top circle. With the needle tool, punch a hole in the semicircle to form the bail. Cut away the excess clay around the edges with the craft knife.

7. Punch a hole in the center of each circle with a drinking straw. Remove the excess clay and remoisten it to be used in another project. Allow the pendant to dry completely.

8. Gently sand the edges of the dry pendant with the emery file. Use the triangle-shaped needle file to get into the small areas around the triangles. Use the half-round needle file to smooth out the edges inside circles. To smooth out the hole in the bail at the top of the pendant, use the round needle file. Use a craft knife to cut away the spaces between the circles and triangle.

9. Fire in activated coconut carbon using the long firing schedule.

Assembling the Necklace

1. After firing, oxidize the pendant. Use a fiber pad to remove a small amount of the surface oxidation. Following the manufacturer's instructions, spray all parts with a flat, clear lacquer to preserve the oxidation.

2. Cut the leather cording to the desired finished length. Open the 5 mm jump ring, and connect it to the bail at the top of the pendant. Close the jump ring securely around the leather cord.

HACIENDA NUMBERS

House numbers don't have to be just utilitarian and limited to what the hardware store has in stock. You can create numbers that complement your home's style and personality, whether it's a contemporary home, Colonial, bungalow, or something in between.

NEEDED

Bronze clay tool kit, page 12

Texture sheet or mold of your choice

Number templates (see below)

Drill bit, 3 mm in diameter

Small mounting nails

TIP

You can draw the address numbers needed by hand onto thick paper or cardstock, or you can print them with a computer. When selecting a word processing font, choose numbers that have smooth edges and aren't too thin. Also, take a look at the font both in normal and in bold type—it can really make a difference. Once you have chosen a font, enlarge the character size so the printed numbers are 4 inches (10.2 cm) tall. For most fonts, this is about a 400-point size. Print the numbers onto thick paper or cardstock. Use scissors to cut out each template.

HERE'S HOW

1. Place a large lump of bronze clay on your work surface. Use the rolling pin to roll a slab that is 10 cards thick. (Roll one slab for each number in the address.)

2. Use a texture sheet or a mold to add texture to the surface of the bronze clay slab/slabs.

3. Position one number template onto the textured clay. Use a craft knife to cut out the number. Repeat this step to cut out all numbers in the address. Let the clay dry naturally.

4. Use an emery file to gently sand the edges of the numbers. Use 400-grit sandpaper to get into any tight corners or angles.

5. Position the bronze clay numbers in the activated coal carbon vertically. Fire the clay in the kiln using the long firing schedule.

6. Determine where to place two holes per house number, and use a permanent marker to mark these locations. (The mounting hardware for the numbers will be inserted through these holes.) Drill the holes, and then use sandpaper or a file to smooth their edges.

7. Finish the numbers as desired (these are polished to a high shine), and then proudly hang your numbers with small mounting nails.

JULIET EARRINGS

Create one-of-a-kind bronze clay beads on cocktail straws, then in assembly-line fashion, join them with delicate twists of wire, stone beads, and pearls for a captivating dangly effect.

NEEDED

- **Bronze clay tool kit, page 12**
- **6 cocktail straws**
- **Block of floral foam**
- **Warming tray or dehydrator**
- **Drill bit, 1 mm in diameter**
- **Chain-nose pliers**
- **Round-nose pliers**
- **Bronze wire, 22-gauge, 3 feet (91.4 cm) long**
- **8 labradorite beads, 4 mm**
- **12 white pearls, 4 mm**
- **Ear wires of your choice**

HERE'S HOW

Creating the Components

1. Prepare an assembly line for the tube beads by applying olive oil to the surface of six cocktail straws. Place a block of florist foam on your workstation. (You'll build the beads on the cocktail straws and prop them in the foam to dry.)

2. Place the fresh bronze clay on your work surface, and roll a slab that is three cards thick.

3. Using the tissue blade, cut a clay rectangle that is 1 x ¾ inch (2.5 x 1.9 cm) long. Position a 1-inch (2.5 cm) side of the rectangle against the straw, and wrap the ¾-inch (1.9 cm) side around the straw (figure 1). Wet and overlap the edges of the clay. Lightly press the edges together so they make full contact with each other. Use the pointed tip of the blending tool to dimple the clay at the seam. This ensures a good bond and adds a decorative edge to the seam. Stick one end of the straw into the florist foam to prop up the bead. This lets the bead dry naturally without any flat spots.

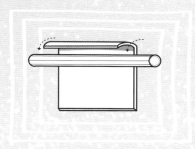

figure 1

4. Repeat steps 2 and 3 to create a total of six tube beads. Let the beads dry to the touch.

5. Slip the beads off the cocktail straws. The inside of the bead will still be moist. Place the beads on a warming tray or dehydrator and let them dry completely.

6. Roll a slab of bronze clay that is four cards thick. Cut two clay strips that each measure 1 x ¼ inch (2.5 cm x 6 mm). Set the strips aside to dry.

7. Smooth the edges of the beads and the slabs with an emery file, and round each corner of the slabs.

8. Find the center of each slab with a ruler. Mark the center points with a pencil. Measure and mark points that are ¼ inch (6 mm) from the center point on both sides (figure 2). Drill holes at each marked point with the drill bit.

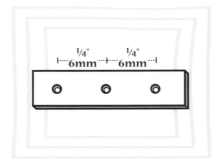

figure 2

9. Place the beads and slabs in the activated coal carbon, and fire them in the kiln using the short firing schedule. Rinse all of the fired pieces in water to remove any residue from the activated carbon. Use a needle tool to remove any carbon particles that are stuck inside the tube beads. Use fine sandpaper to create a satin finish on each bead and slab.

Assembling the Earrings

1. Cut six pieces of wire, each 2¼ inches (5.7 cm) long. Wire wrap a loop at the end of each piece.

2. Add one pearl, one labradorite bead, and one bronze clay tube bead to each wire.

3. Run one of the beaded wires through the center hole in one of the slabs, then wire wrap it closed.

4. Pass the other wires through the outside holes of the slab and use the chain-nose pliers to create tight spirals at the end of the wire.

5. Make six spiral end head pins. Add accent beads to the end of each and wire wrap to the bottom of each bead assembly.

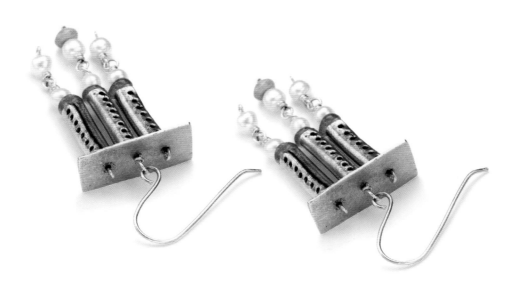

ARROWHEAD PENDANT

While researching the history of bronze, I stumbled across pictures of ancient tools and weapons. This arrowhead is similar in design to one from the Bronze Age.

NEEDED

- Bronze clay tool kit, page 12
- Photocopied template, page 122
- Bronze slip
- Drill bit, 1.5 mm
- Ammonia
- Salt
- Spray lacquer fixative
- Beading wire
- Bronze or brass spacer beads
- Lapis beads, 3 mm
- Crimp beads
- Clasp, commercial or handmade

HERE'S HOW

1. Place the bronze clay on the work surface. Use the rolling pin to roll the clay into a slab that is three cards thick. Use the template to cut two teardrop shapes from the clay slab. Each teardrop should measure approximately 1 inch (2.5 cm) long x ½ inch (1.3 cm) wide at its widest point. Cut one of the teardrops in half lengthwise with a craft knife. Let the teardrop forms dry.

2. Sand the front and back surfaces of the full teardrop shape with sandpaper. Use the emery file to file the flat sides of the half-teardrop pieces.

3. Brush a thick stripe of slip down the center of the full teardrop shape, from the tip to the bottom edge. Place one of the half-teardrop pieces vertically onto the slip (figure 1). Use the blending tool to blend in any excess slip. Allow the slip to dry completely. Inspect the seams where the forms come together, and fill in any gaps with additional slip. Repeat this step on the opposite side of the form.

4. Once the pieces have been assembled and dried, use fine sandpaper to sand away any excess slip from the seams.

5. To create the shank of the arrowhead, roll a piece of clay into a log shape that is approximately ½ inch (1.3 cm) long x ¼ inch (6 mm) in diameter. Use the craft knife to make two incisions on one end of the shank, each approximately ⅛ inch (3 mm) deep (figure 2).

slip

figure 1

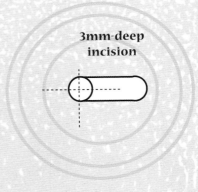

3mm-deep incision

figure 2

6. Place the arrowhead into the incisions made in the log, nestling it into the cuts (figure 3). Use the blending tool to smooth the shank into the arrowhead blades. Set aside the arrowhead to dry.

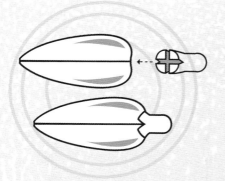

figure 3

7. When the piece is completely dry, use the emery file and sandpaper to smooth the shank of the arrowhead. Use the drill bit to bore a hole in the shank of the arrowhead, approximately ¼ inch (6 mm) in from the end.

8. Place the arrowhead in the coal activated carbon, and fire it in the kiln following the long firing schedule. Thoroughly clean the pendant after firing.

9. Pack salt onto the entire surface of the arrowhead. Place the arrowhead into a sealable container next to a bowl of ammonia. Allow the arrowhead to fume for several days to produce a blue-green patina (see page 25 for detailed information). Sand its fins with sandpaper to allow some of the bronze color to show through the blue patina. Seal the oxidation with lacquer.

10. String the arrowhead onto beading wire along with the 3 mm lapis beads. Use crimp beads and a clasp to complete the necklace.

TRIBECA BELT BUCKLE

This buckle design is accomplished by carving strips out of a texture sheet before pressing it into the clay. It's so easy that the most challenging part is soldering the findings in place.

NEEDED

Bronze clay tool kit, page 12

Oval template, 3 x 4 inches (7.6 x 10.2 cm)

Texture sheet of your choice

Bronze slip

Belt buckle findings (loop and peg)

Easy silver solder

Basic soldering setup

Bronze oxidizer

HERE'S HOW

1. Place a large lump of bronze clay on your work surface. Use the rolling pin to roll a slab that is four cards thick.

2. Position the oval template on the rolled out clay. Use the craft knife to cut around the oval template. (This is the base of the belt buckle.) Set aside the clay oval, and cover it with plastic wrap.

3. Place a lump of bronze clay on your work surface. Use the rolling pin to roll a slab that is three cards thick.

4. Use the texture sheet to texture the surface of the clay slab. Use a craft knife to cut out several curved strips from the textured sheet. (The project shown here features seven strips.)

5. Remove the plastic wrap from the belt buckle base, and determine where the strip embellishments will be placed.

6. Using the blending tool, add slip to the belt buckle base where one decorative strip will be placed. Lay the strip onto the slip, and gently press it into place. Wipe away any excess slip from the seams with a blending tool. Use a craft knife to trim away the portion of the strip that overhangs the oval base. Repeat this step with the remaining strips. Allow the clay buckle to completely dry naturally.

7. Use the emery file to sand the edges of the dry buckle smooth.

8. Place the buckle in activated coconut carbon. Fire it using the long firing schedule.

9. Thoroughly rinse the fired buckle, and make certain that no carbon residue is left on its surface.

10. Solder the belt buckle findings (loop and peg) onto the back of the buckle with easy silver solder. Oxidize the buckle with the bronze oxidizer, and then polish it to bring out the detail in the texture.

ILLUMINATION VESSEL

This project is ideal when you're ready to begin working with large pieces of bronze clay. Designed to hold a votive candle, this container is also perfect for pocket change or jewelry.

NEEDED

- Bronze clay tool kit, page 12
- Foam ball, 3 inches (7.6 cm) in diameter
- Toothpicks
- Candle wax
- Texture sheets
- 3-inch (7.6 cm) diameter circle template
- Bronze slip
- Spray lacquer

figure 1

HERE'S HOW

1. To prepare the foam ball, place three toothpicks into its base at an angle, forming support legs. Melt the candle wax according to the manufacturer's instructions. Dip the foam ball into the melted wax, coating half of the ball. Let the wax solidify on the ball, and then dip it a second time. The wax will fill the holes in the foam, creating a smooth surface. Once the wax is completely solid, rub some oil onto the surface. This will prevent the clay from sticking to the wax.

2. Roll a large amount of fresh bronze clay into a slab that is four cards thick. Texture the clay with a texture sheet. Place the 3-inch (7.6 cm) diameter template on the clay, and use the needle tool to cut out the circle.

3. Drape the clay circle, texture side out, on the wax portion of the foam ball. Press the clay onto the ball so it is completely touching the form. Set the form aside, and let the clay dry.

4. Remove the dry clay bowl from the foam ball. Use the emery file to smooth the edge of the bowl. Then, use the fiber sanding pad to further smooth and round the edge.

5. Place the bowl upside down on your work surface. Find the center of the textured side of the bowl. Use a pencil to draw a small circle at this point.

6. Roll a thick coil of clay, and form it into a ring. Trim the ends of the coil, and use the blending tool to smooth the joint.

7. With the paintbrush, wet the area of the bowl that was marked in step 5. Allow the water to soak into the clay. Add thick slip to the wet area. Pick up the coil ring, place it onto the slip, and press it into position (figure 1). Use the blending tool to smooth any excess slip into the seam where the bowl meets the ring. Let the ring and slip dry completely.

8. After the ring is dry, inspect the inside and outside seams where the bowl meets the ring. Add more slip to reinforce the seam and the joint in the ring. Let the slip dry completely.

9. File the bottom of the ring so it sits flat. Use the fiber pad to smooth the surface of the ring. Place the candleholder vertically in the activated coal carbon. (This will prevent the clay from slumping during firing.) Fire the candleholder in the kiln following the long firing schedule.

10. Remove the candleholder from the carbon, and rinse it in water to remove any carbon dust. Leave the metal surface the color it is straight out of the kiln. To preserve the color, spray the surface with clear lacquer and let dry.

BOLO REVOLUTION

Random fact: The bolo is the official state tie of New Mexico. Fashion fact: They're not just for men anymore! Small coils, balls, and teardrop shaped bits of clay are transformed into a flower with the help of a needle tool.

NEEDED

Bronze clay tool kit, page 12

Photocopied template, page 122

Bronze slip

Cellophane tape

Circle template

Bronze or brass wire, 12 gauge,
    3 inches (7.6 cm)

Basic soldering kit, page 7

Hard silver solder

Medium silver solder

Bronze oxidizer

Clear spray lacquer sealer

5-minute epoxy

Bolo cord, 36 inches (91.4 cm)

HERE'S HOW

Making the Bolo

1. Place the bronze clay on your work surface, and roll a slab that is four cards thick. Use the photocopied template and a needle tool to cut out the bolo base.

2. With your fingers, roll a coil of bronze clay on your work surface. This coil will be placed along the edge of the bolo, as a border. Use a paintbrush to wet the perimeter of the bolo. Place the coil on the wet surface, and press it into place with your fingers. Let the bolo dry completely. With the emery file, sand all edges of the bolo smooth.

3. To form the flower petals, roll several pieces of clay into narrow teardrop shapes, each approximately ¹⁄₂ inch (1.3 cm) long. Place the petals under plastic wrap to keep them moist.

4. With a wet paintbrush, add water to the area of the bolo where you wish to place the flower. Let the water soak in so the surface becomes moist, and then paint some slip onto the moist surface. Attach the petals one at a time, lightly pressing each into the slip. When all the petals are in place, wick water around the edges of the petals with a wet paintbrush to make a strong bond between the petals and the slip.

5. Create lines in each of the flower petals with the needle tool. Pinch a small amount of bronze clay, and roll it into a ball. Press the ball into the center of the flower.

6. Use a paintbrush to draw a line of water down the center of the bolo where you wish to place the flower stem. After the water soaks into the surface, apply some slip on the moist surface exactly where the flower

stem will be placed. Use your fingertips to roll a bronze clay snake on your work surface. Gently pick up the snake and place it onto the slip. Blend in any excess slip with the blending tool.

7. Apply some slip on either side of the stem where the leaves will be placed. Roll two pieces of bronze clay into long leaf shapes. Press the leaves into the slip. Wick water around the edges of the leaves with the paintbrush. Make veins in the surface of the leaves with the needle tool.

8. Let the bolo dry completely. Use the fine sandpaper to sand the entire surface of the bolo.

Making the Tips

1. Cut two pieces of paper, and form them into cones that each measure 3 inches (7.6 cm) long, with a ½-inch-wide (1.3 cm) opening. Use tape to hold the papers in the cone shape.

2. Roll a slab of bronze clay that is two cards thick. Use the circle template and a needle tool to cut out a clay circle that is 1¾ inches (4.4 cm) in diameter. Lift the circle and wrap it around one of the paper forms to create a cone. Use a paintbrush to add water to the clay where it overlaps. Also brush some water into the seam to make sure the clay sticks to itself. Add decorative elements to the cone if desired. I added a snake of clay around the circumference of the tip. Set the cone aside to dry. Repeat this step to create the second clay cone.

3. Let both clay cones dry completely. Check the seams on both cones, fill any gaps with slip, and let the slip dry. Use the emery file to smooth the edges of the dry cones.

Firing & Finishing

1. Place the bolo and the pair of tips into either activated coconut or coal carbon. Fire the pieces in the kiln following the long firing schedule. After firing, rinse the pieces in water and dry them completely.

2. To make the bolo back, form the 3-inch (7.6 cm) piece of 12-gauge bronze or brass wire into a figure-eight shape (figure 1). Solder together the ends of the wire using hard silver solder.

figure 1

3. Bend up the circle portions of the figure-eight piece (figure 2). Using medium silver solder, solder the bolo back into place.

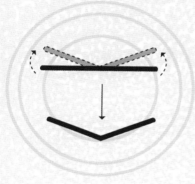

figure 2

4. Oxidize the bolo and tips to create an antique appearance. Use fine sandpaper to remove the oxidation from the surface of the bronze.

5. Lace the 36-inch-long (91.4 cm) bolo cord through the bolo back. Mix the epoxy and apply it to the ends of the bolo cord. Adhere one bronze clay tip to each end of the cord. Let the epoxy dry completely.

CORAL COLLAR

Emulate the provocative shapes and textures of coral through sculpting and carving bronze clay. Thick branches of real and simulated coral can be found at most bead shops and jewelry suppliers.

NEEDED

Bronze clay kit, page 12

Drill bit, 1.5 mm in diameter

Pin vise

Bronze oxidizer

Rotary tumbler

Stainless steel shot

Burnishing compound

Stringing wire

Coral branch beads

Small white pearl spacer beads

Crimp beads

Clasp of your choice

figure 1

HERE'S HOW

1. Roll a marble-sized lump of clay into a log that is approximately 2¼ inches (5.7 cm) long by ³⁄₈ inch (1 cm) thick. The log should be uneven with blunt ends.

2. Using the craft knife, make a small slice anywhere on the surface of the log. With the rubber blending tool, form the cut clay into a round branchlike shape. Make one to three additional slices on the log and shape it (figure 1). Once the branch has been formed to your liking, create slight bends in it for a more organic feel.

3. Repeat steps 1 and 2 to make several branch beads, each one slightly different from the others. Dry the branch beads completely. Refine the beads with fine sandpaper to remove any fingerprints.

4. Mount the drill bit in the pin vise. Drill a hole approximately ¼ inch (6 mm) from the top edge of each bead. (**Note:** *Let the drill bit do the work. There's no need to put too much pressure on it.*) The coral that inspired these beads has a small dimple at each end of the branch. To replicate this, use the drill bit to create a small divot at each end of each bead.

5. Place the beads in the activated coconut carbon, and fire them in the kiln on the long firing schedule. Following the manufacturer's instructions, oxidize the fired beads to bring out their surface texture. Remove the oxidation from the highest levels with sandpaper. Tumble the beads in a rotary tumbler to bring them to a high shine.

6. Cut a piece of stringing wire that is 3 inches (7.6 cm) longer than the desired finished length of your necklace. Attach one part of the clasp onto one end of the wire with a crimp bead. String the coral beads and pearls onto the wire, interspersing the bronze beads throughout the strand. Once you reach the end of the strand, attach the other end of the clasp with a crimp bead.

COASTERS DEL SOL

Set down your cold drinks in style. With bronze clay, you can work larger than ever before, and this is the perfect project to get you started.

NEEDED

- **Bronze clay tool kit, page 12**
- **Texture sheet with shallow design**
- **Bronze slip**
- **Warming tray**
- **Steel bench block or anvil**
- **Rawhide mallet**
- **Spray lacquer or sealer, glossy or matte**
- **Thin corkboard**
- **5-minute clear epoxy**

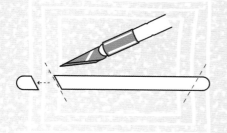

figure 1

HERE'S HOW

1. Place a large lump of clay on your work surface. Use the rolling pin to roll a slab that is five cards thick. Select a texture sheet with a shallow design. (If the texture is too deep the surface of the coaster will be uneven and could possibly result in spilled drinks. And nobody likes that!) Oil the surface of the texture sheet. Place it on the slab of clay, and press it into the surface.

2. With the tissue blade, cut the textured clay into a 4½-inch (11.4 cm) square. Let the clay dry naturally. If it's dried too quickly, the clay may warp. If it does warp, the clay is still flexible after drying and can be pressed flat. Use the emery file to sand the edges smooth.

3. Roll four logs of clay on the work surface, each ⅛ inch (3 mm) in diameter. Trim the ends of the logs at an angle (figure 1). Place the logs under the plastic wrap to keep them moist.

4. With the blending tool, apply slip to one edge of the textured side of the coaster. Press one of the logs into place. Repeat this step on the three remaining edges of the coaster.

5. Wet the paintbrush and wick water around the inside seams. Smooth any excess slip with the

blending tool. To reinforce the corners, use the blending tool to add slip to the seams. Place the coaster on a warming tray to dry the additional clay and slip. Use the emery file to sand the edges and bottom of the coaster.

6. Place the coaster flat in the activated coal carbon, and fire it in the kiln using the long firing schedule. If the coaster warps during firing, place it on a steel bench block or anvil and use a rawhide mallet to flatten it.

7. Lightly finish the surface of the coaster with the fine sandpaper. This will bring out the highlights of the texture, leaving the kiln patina in the recesses. Seal the surface of the coaster with lacquer.

8. Use sandpaper to create a rough surface on the bottom of the coaster. This will produce tooth for the glue to hold on to.

9. Using scissors, cut the corkboard to match the size of the coaster. Apply the epoxy to the corkboard, place the bronze coaster onto the cork, and press into place. Wipe away any excess epoxy that oozes out the edges. Let the epoxy cure according to the manufacturer's directions.

MILAGRO CHARMS

Milagro means miracle in Spanish. Often used on altars and shrines, milagros can also be worn or carried for good luck. Every milagro has a different meaning, and each charm is open to the wearer's interpretation.

NEEDED

Bronze clay tool kit, page 12

Photocopied templates, page 123

Assorted needle files

Drill bit, 1.5 mm

8 jump rings, 20-gauge, each 4 mm in diameter

Charm bracelet chain with clasp, commercial or handmade

MAKE YOUR OWN MIRACLES

Here are meanings for the milagros I used on my bracelet. Of course, these are open to interpretation. And you don't have to stop here. Milagros are personal and can be represented by all sorts of things: a mouth, a body, an animal—you name it!

Heart – Love

Eyes – Watching, being watched over

Arm – Strength, work, embrace

Leg – Strength, travel, journey

Head – Mind or spirit

House – Home

Hen – Mothering

Ear – Hearing

HERE'S HOW

1. Cut out the photocopied design template for each charm. (Each template includes a ring at the top for attaching the charms later on.) Place the bronze clay on your work surface, and roll a slab that is five cards thick.

2. Lay one charm template on the slab, and use the needle tool to cut around the perimeter. Repeat this process for each milagro design. Let the charms dry completely.

3. With a pencil, draw details onto the various milagro charms. To scratch the designs into the clay, trace your pencil markings with the needle tool. You may need to make several passes with the needle tool to create lines that are deep enough to stand out on the charm after firing.

4. Smooth the edges of each charm with the emery file and needle files. With the drill bit, create a hole in the center of the top of the charm for the jump ring.

5. Place the charms in the activated coal carbon. Fire the charms in the kiln using the short firing schedule.

6. Sand the fired charms with fine sandpaper. Use the polishing cloth to bring a soft sheen to the surface of the charms.

7. Lay the charms out on your work surface, and determine what order you want them to be attached to the bracelet.

8. Open one jump ring, and attach a charm. Connect the jump ring to the charm bracelet securely. Repeat this step to connect all charms and complete the bracelet.

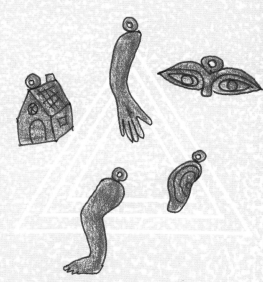

EVOLUTION HOOPS

Together, bronze and silver metal clay form a dynamic duo. You'll make the dangles quickly and simply, and then hammer away at the handmade hoops.

Bronze clay tool kit, page 12

Silver metal clay (low shrink)

Two different texture sheets

Liver of sulfur

Bronze oxidizer

20-gauge round sterling silver wire

Round-nose pliers

Cup bur, 1 mm

Bench block

Chasing hammer

Chain-nose pliers

Round nose pliers

Flush cutters

Round needle file

Making the Silver Elements

Note: *You are making the silver metal clay pieces first to reduce the possibility of cross contamination. If silver metal clay has bronze clay in it, the bronze can possibly harm the sintering process of the silver clay. To prevent this, make sure your work surface, texture sheets, and other tools are clean and free of any bronze clay debris.*

1. Roll a silver metal clay slab that is three cards thick. Texture the clay slab with one of the texture sheets. Cut two clay rectangles from the textured slab, each measuring 1 x ¾ inches (2.5 x 1.9 cm). Use the needle tool to create a hole centered near the top of each rectangle. Let the clay dry completely.

2. Sand the edges of the dry clay smooth with the emery file. Refine and enlarge the holes at the top of the forms with the round needle file.

3. Fire the silver metal clay in the kiln according to the manufacturer's directions.

Making the Bronze Elements

1. Place the bronze clay on your clean work surface, and roll a slab that is three cards thick. Select the second texture sheet, and press it into the surface of the clay. Cut two rectangles from the textured slab, each measuring 1½ x ¾ inches (3.8 x 1.9 cm). Use the needle tool to create a hole centered near the top of each rectangle. Let the clay dry completely.

2. Use the emery file to smooth the edges of each bronze clay rectangle. Smooth and enlarge the holes in the top of each rectangle with the round needle file.

3. Place the bronze clay pieces in the activated coal carbon, and fire them in the kiln using the short firing schedule.

Finishing & Assembling the Hoops

1. Oxidize all four metal pieces, using liver of sulfur for the silver, and bronze oxidizer for the bronze clay. Use a polishing cloth to remove excess oxidation from the high points of the textured surfaces.

2. To make the ear hoops, cut two pieces of 20-gauge wire, each 2 inches (5 cm) long. Use the round-nose pliers to make an eye at one end of each wire. Use the cup bur to smooth the other wire ends. (This is the part of the earring that will go through your ear.) Bend each wire around a mandrel or a marker into a hoop shape measuring between ¾ and 1 inch (1.9 and 2.5 cm) in diameter. One at a time, place each hoop on the bench block and lightly hammer it to create texture.

3. Slide one bronze rectangle and one silver rectangle onto each hoop. Use the chain-nose pliers to make a slight bend approximately 4 mm from the end of the wire. To secure the earring, insert this bend through the eye on the opposite end of the hoop.

SERPENTINE RING

Throughout history, the spiral has been a powerful symbol. Coils are attached to a simple band that you'll make two and a half sizes larger than the desired size to allow for clay shrinkage.

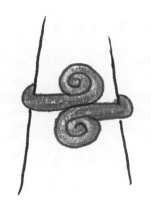

NEEDED

Bronze clay tool kit, page 12

Ring mandrel

Plastic wrap

Bronze slip

Bronze oxidizer

Paint-on clear lacquer sealer

HERE'S HOW

Determining the Size of the Ring

1. To compensate for the shrinkage of the clay, the ring will be built 2½ sizes larger than the desired size. For example, if the final ring should be a size 6, you will need to build a size 8½.

2. Cut a strip of paper approximately ¼ inch (6 mm) wide by 3 inches (7.6 cm) long. Wrap the strip around the ring mandrel so it's 2½ sizes larger than the necessary size. Mark the strip where the paper overlaps. Add 4 mm to this length. (This additional amount compensates for the thickness of the clay and allows for the ends to be overlapped.)

Forming, Firing, and Finishing the Ring

1. Use your hands to roll a fresh piece of bronze clay into a log shape that is approximately 2 inches (5 cm) long by ¼ inch (6 mm) thick. Place the log on the oiled work surface, and use the rolling pin to roll it six cards thick. The rolled clay should be long enough to fit the template.

2. Use the tissue blade to cut the rolled clay 5 mm wide (figure 1). Lay the paper template on the rolled clay. Use the tissue blade to cut the clay to the determined length. Remove the paper template from the clay.

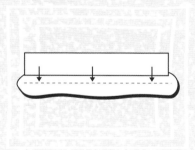

figure 1

3. Wrap the ring mandrel with plastic wrap to prevent the clay from sticking to it. Gently lift the strip of clay off the work surface. Wrap the strip around the plastic-covered ring mandrel at the previously determined size. Overlap the ends of the strip by at least 1 mm.

4. With the paintbrush, apply a small amount of water to wet the seam. Using the blending tool, blend the seam together until it disappears. Be careful not to use too much pressure as the seam is blended. This could result in stretching the ring and changing its size.

5. Let the ring partially dry on the ring mandrel. When the ring is dry enough to support itself, slide the plastic wrap off the mandrel. The ring will come off the mandrel with the plastic. Remove the plastic wrap from the inside of the ring. Place the ring on a drying tray, and allow it to dry completely.

6. To blend the seam inside the ring, roll a small, thin coil of clay in your fingers. Wet the inside seam with the paintbrush. Press the small coil of clay in the seam. Blend the wet clay into the seam with the blending tool. If necessary, apply some thick slip to the seam also, and blend it in until the seam disappears. Set the ring aside to dry.

7. Note: *When sanding the ring, make sure to fully support it with your fingertips. If the ring is unsupported, it could possibly break as it is being filed.* Gently sand the edges of the dry ring with the emery file. Roll up a piece of the sanding pad, and use it to sand inside the ring.

Inspect the seam, inside and outside. If you see any gaps, apply more slip and let the clay dry before sanding it again.

8. Roll a pea-sized piece of fresh clay into a thin snake that is 2 to 3 inches (5 to 7.6 cm) long, tapering the ends as you roll. The longer the snake is rolled, the larger the ring's coil will be. It's no big deal if the coil isn't totally symmetrical. In fact, an uneven coil adds to the charm of the ring.

9. Brush water onto the surface of the snake with the paintbrush. With your fingertips, begin coiling the snake into an S shape. Turn each end of the snake in opposite directions (figure 2).

figure 2

10. Add slip to the ring band at the blended seam. Place the S-shaped coil onto the slip. Gently press the coil into place so it is in full contact with the ring band. Let the ring dry completely. Smooth away any marks or fingerprints on the coil with fine sandpaper.

11. Place the ring in the activated coal carbon, and fire it in the kiln following the long firing schedule. After firing, rinse the ring in water to remove any residue left from the activated carbon.

12. Following the manufacturer's instructions, oxidize the ring to give it an antique patina. Use fine sandpaper to remove the oxidation from the high points on the ring. Also sand inside the band. Paint the inside and outside of the ring with lacquer to seal the finish.

MAYAN HOOPS

These bronze beauties reflect light and warmth with your every step. Make the triangular cutouts quickly and consistently using a transformed cocktail straw.

Bronze clay tool kit, page 12

Circle template, 1⅝ inches (4.1 cm) in diameter

Circle template, ¾ inch (1.9 cm) in diameter

Cocktail straw

Drinking straw

Triangle needle file

Drill bit, 1.5 mm in diameter

Bronze slip

Rotary tumbler

Stainless steel shot

Burnishing compound

Gold-filled wire, 20-gauge, 6-inch (15.2 cm) length

Wire cutters

Round-nose pliers

Cup bur, 1 mm in diameter

Chain-nose pliers

1. It's easiest to construct one earring at a time. Place the bronze clay on your work surface, and roll a slab that is five cards thick. Use a circle template to cut one circle that is 1⅝ inches (4.1 cm) in diameter. To form the crescent shape, use a ¾-inch (1.9 cm) circle template to cut away the upper portion of the larger clay circle (figure 1).

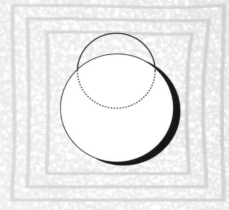

figure 1

2. Form one end of a cocktail straw into a triangle with your fingers (figure 2). Use the bent straw to cut triangles along the outside edge of the clay crescent. Keep the bottom edge of each triangle approximately 2 mm away from the edge of the crescent. Use the needle tool to poke a hole in one corner of the crescent. (This will hold the wrapped ear wire.) Let the earring dry while you repeat steps 1 and 2 to construct the second earring.

figure 2

3. Roll a small slab of clay five cards thick. Use a drinking straw to cut two circles from the clay. With the needle tool, pierce a hole in the center of each circle. Set the circles aside to dry.

4. Once all clay pieces are dry, file one point of each crescent flat (the point that doesn't have the hole). Refine the triangle cutouts with a triangle-shaped needle file. Use the drill bit or the round needle file to enlarge the pierced hole in the center of each small circle and the pierced hole in the corner of each earring. Sand a flat edge on each small circle. Finally, use the emery file to smooth all edges of all the earring components.

5. Apply a small amount of thick slip to the flat edge of one of the circles. Place the circle on the filed edge of the crescent, perpendicular to the earring (figure 3). Press the circle onto the edge, and allow the slip to dry. Inspect the joint and fill in any gaps with additional slip. Gently file where the circle and crescent join.

6. To prevent the earrings from warping, stand them vertically in the activated coconut carbon. Fire the earrings in the kiln using the short firing schedule.

7. Tumble the fired earrings in a rotary tumbler for 30 minutes to polish them.

8. Cut two 3-inch (7.6 cm) pieces of wire. Make a loop in one end of the wire with round-nose pliers. Feed the loop through the hole at the tip of the crescent. Use chain-nose pliers to wrap the wire around itself, securing it through the hole. Smooth and round the loose end of the wire with the cup bur. Use chain-nose pliers to make a 45° bend approximately 5 mm in from the loose end of the wire. Use your fingers to shape the remaining wire into a soft arc. This positions the 45° bend close to the circle on the tip of the earring. The bend fits into the circle to secure the earring. Repeat this process to make the ear wire for the second earring.

figure 3

CUSTOM PET TAGS

Size and style a custom tag to suit your animal companion. Miniature cookie cutters make it easy and are available in almost every shape imaginable.

NEEDED

Bronze clay tool kit, page 12

Alphabet stamps, optional

Miniature cookie cutter, dog bone or shape of your choice

Drill bit, 1.5 mm

Rotary tumbler

Jump ring, 18 gauge, 5 mm in diameter

OTHER IDEAS

To give the tag a personal feel, why not handwrite your pet's name directly in the clay? After stamping out the shape, allow the clay to dry completely. Lightly write the name on the tag with a pencil. Trace your writing with a needle tool. (You may need to go over the writing a couple of times to make the lines deep enough to be visible after firing.) Once you are happy with the depth of the letters, finish and fire as directed above.

HERE'S HOW

1. Select the letter stamps you need to spell your pet's name. Place the bronze clay on your work surface, and roll a slab that is four cards thick.

2. Use the miniature cookie cutter to cut out the shape of your pet tag. Stamp the name into the center of the wet clay. Let the tag dry completely.

3. Use emery files to sand the edges of the tag smooth. Find the center of the tag, and mark it with a pencil approximately 3 mm in from the top edge. Use the drill bit to make a hole through the tag at the marked point.

4. Position the tag in the activated coconut carbon, and fire it in the kiln using the standard firing schedule.

5. Place the tag in a rotary tumbler, and tumble it for 1 hour to bring the metal to a high shine.

6. Add a jump ring to the tag, and attach it to your pet's collar. There you have it—doggie couture!

HAMMERED AMULET

Big and bold, this attractive pendant demands attention. It's also deceivingly easy to make—you create its robust texture without ever picking up a hammer!

NEEDED

Bronze clay tool kit, page 12

Drinking straw

Bronze slip

Oxidizing solution

Polishing cloth

Chain or cord of your choice

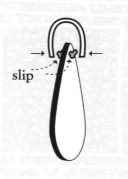

slip

figure 1

HERE'S HOW

1. Place the bronze clay on your work surface, and roll a slab that is five cards thick. Use a craft knife to cut out a teardrop shape that is 2½ inches (6.4 cm) long and 1¾ inches (4.4 cm) at the widest part.

2. Select a tool that has a smooth rounded end. (For this pendant, I used the handle end of a blending tool.) Create a dimpled texture by repeatedly pressing the end of the tool over the entire surface of the clay. For an authentic hammered look, allow the dimples to overlap. Let the textured clay dry completely.

3. To construct the bail, roll a narrow slab of bronze clay that is three cards thick. Use a craft knife to cut a 1¼ x ¼-inch (3.2 cm x 6 mm) rectangle. Slightly curve the short edges of the rectangle. Drape the rectangle into a U-shape over a drinking straw. Let the clay dry completely.

4. Refine the edges of the teardrop pendant with an emery file. Gently remove the bail from the straw. Using a very light touch, sand all edges of the bail with the emery file.

5. Apply thick slip to the tip of the pendant on both the front and back sides. Place the bail over the slip, and pinch it into place (figure 1). Smooth excess slip with the rubber blending tool. Using the paintbrush, wick a tiny amount of water around the seam where the bail and pendant meet.

6. Roll a pinch of bronze clay into a ball that is approximately ⅛ inch (3 mm) in diameter. Place some slip on the front side of the bail, above its bottom edge. Position the ball on the slip, and smooth into place. Let the slip dry completely.

7. Place the pendant in the activated coal carbon, and fire it in the kiln following the long firing schedule.

8. Following the manufacturer's instructions, immerse the fired pendant into an oxidizing solution. Once the desired patina is achieved, remove the pendant from the oxidizer, and rinse well.

9. Rub a polishing cloth over the surface of the pendant to remove the oxidation from the high points of the hammered texture. String the pendant on the chain or cord of your choice.

LAVA BEADS

This lightweight piece replicates the distinctive texture of lava rock. Use a two-part molding compound to easily capture the unique surface texture.

NEEDED

Bronze clay tool kit, page 12

Lava rocks, various shapes and sizes

Two-part mold compound

Bronze slip

Drill bit, 2.5 mm in diameter

Pin vise

4 mm round beads

49-strand bronze colored beading wire

Clasp of your choice

Making the Mold

1. Select a rock to mold. Using a permanent marker, draw a line around the edge of the rock that bisects it into halves. This line will help you when you place the rock into the mold compound.

2. To make the bottom half of the mold, first mix the mold compound according to the manufacturer's directions. Form the compound into a patty that is about twice as thick as the rock. Press the rock into the compound, up to the line drawn in step 1. Let the compound set, leaving the rock in the compound.

3. Mix a second batch of mold compound, and press it onto the other half of the rock. Make certain that the top half makes full contact with the bottom half of the mold. Let the second batch of compound set completely, then pry apart the two mold halves and remove the rock.

Making the Beads

1. Roll a lump of bronze clay into a slab that is three cards thick. Press the slab of clay into one half of the mold. Use the craft knife to cut away any excess clay, taking care not to cut into the mold. Repeat this step to roll and press clay into the other half of the mold.

2. Place both halves of the molded clay into a food dehydrator, and let them dry completely. Remove the dried clay from the molds, and sand the edges of each half with the emery file. As you are sanding, spot check to make sure the edges of the two sides match up.

3. Wet each matching sanded edge with a paintbrush. Apply thick slip around the edge of one of the halves with the rubber blending tool. Press the other half of the bead into the slip. Smooth away any excess slip with the blending tool. Let the slip dry completely.

4. Inspect the seam of the bead for any gaps or cracks, and fill them with more slip. When all gaps have been filled and the slip is dry, very gently sand the edges with fine sandpaper.

5. Use a marker to mark two points, one on each side of the bead, where the holes are to be placed. Drill holes at the marked points with the drill bit secured in the pin vise. If the seam splits after drilling, fill the gap with more slip, and let dry.

6. Repeat steps 1 through 5 as often as needed to make as many beads as you like.

Firing & Finishing

1. Place the beads vertically in the activated coal carbon so the beads won't cave in during the firing. Fire the beads in the kiln following the long firing schedule.

2. Use a fiber pad to bring the surface of the fired beads to a satin finish. String all the beads together using the round beads as accents. Use crimp beads and a clasp to complete the necklace.

DIA DE LOS MUERTOS

Throughout the Mexican celebration known as Dia de los Muertos (Day of the Dead), colorful flowers are used to honor one's ancestors. These bright festival bouquets inspired the painted accents on this lucky charm.

NEEDED

Bronze clay tool kit, page 12

Photocopied template, page 122

Pencil with unused eraser

Bronze slip

Cocktail straw

Bronze oxidizer

Acrylic model paint in assorted colors

Spray gloss sealant

HERE'S HOW

Making the Pendant

1. Make a ball of clay that is approximately the size of a large coin. Roll it out so it's five cards thick. Place the photocopied template on the clay slab, and cut out the skull shape with a needle tool. Very lightly, press around the edges of the skull with your fingertips to give the clay a slightly rounded appearance.

2. Now, add the features to the face. Press the eye sockets into the skull with the eraser end of a pencil. To form the nostrils (under the eyes), press the tip of the blending tool into the clay at an angle. Use the needle tool to mark a horizontal line in the jaw area. Finally, to form teeth, use a needle tool to score several vertical lines through the mouth.

3. Let the skull dry completely. Smooth and round the edges with an emery file.

4. Wet the area with a paintbrush where the flowers and vines will be placed. Roll a small amount of fresh clay into a thin coil. Place the coil on the wet area of the skull, and arrange it into a vinelike shape. Use this method to create two or three vines on the skull.

5. To form the flower petals, roll a small amount of clay into a ball with your fingers. Flatten the ball between your thumb and forefinger, and then pinch one end to form a teardrop shape. Each flower will have five petals, so make a total of 15 petals for three flowers. Place the petals under plastic wrap to keep them moist so they will be easy to apply to the skull.

6. Brush some slip onto the area where water was previously applied. Press each petal into the slip to form three flowers. Roll three extra-small balls of clay with your fingers.

Press one ball into the center of each flower. If necessary, brush the whole flower arrangement with a small amount of water to guarantee that all pieces have adhered to the skull. (Brushing with water will also help remove any fingerprints left in the clay.) Let the pendant dry completely.

Making & Attaching the Tube Bail

1. Oil the surface of a cocktail straw. Roll some fresh clay that is two cards thick. Cut a strip of clay that is 1 inch (2.5 cm) wide. Roll the strip around the cocktail straw, allowing the ends to overlap. Cut away any excess clay if necessary. Wet the seam, and use the blending tool to blend the seam smoothly. Allow the bail to dry completely.

2. Remove the straw from the bail. Sand its edges with the emery file, and then lightly sand one side of the bail to create a flat spot (figure 1). This is the area where the bail will attach to the pendant.

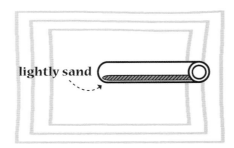

lightly sand

figure 1

3. Use the blending tool to apply a thick layer of slip to the bail where it has been filed flat. Press the bail (slip side down) onto the pendant, approximately 1/2 inch (1.3 cm) down from the top edge. Use the blending tool to smooth out any excess slip from around the edges of the bail. Let the slip dry.

4. Check the seams where the bail and pendant meet. If there is a gap, fill it with slip and let dry. When the seams are dry, use the emery file to do any final refining on the pendant.

Firing, Finishing, and Painting

1. Place the pendant in either activated coconut or coal carbon, and fire it in a kiln using the long firing schedule.

2. Following the manufacturer's instructions, oxidize the pendant to bring out the details. Use fine sandpaper to remove oxidation from the high points of the surface. Rinse the pendant in water to remove any residue left from sanding.

3. Paint colors onto the flowers and vines with model paint and a fine brush. Allow the paint to dry completely. Once dry, spray the entire surface with a coat of clear gloss sealant.

PAISLEY BROOCH

Painting fired bronze clay with model acrylics is
a simple way to add a splash of color. Attaching
the pin back with solder elevates this brooch to
an advanced project.

NEEDED

HERE'S HOW

1. Place the bronze clay on your work surface, and roll a slab that is five cards thick. Place the photocopied paisley template on the clay slab. Use the needle tool to cut out the paisley, including the small interior shape near its tail. Allow the brooch to dry completely.

2. Use the emery file to smooth the edges of the brooch. Use the round needle file to smooth inside the interior shape.

3. Roll a fresh, pea-sized piece of clay into a long thin snake. Use a paintbrush to wet the surface of the snake. Add water to the perimeter of the brooch, about $\frac{1}{4}$ inch (6 mm) inside its edge. Allow the water to soak into the surface of the clay. Add a layer of slip to the area where the water was applied. Gently lift the clay snake and place it on the moistened area of the brooch. Use the paintbrush to position the snake. Cut away any excess clay with a craft knife, and then pat the snake into place with a paintbrush. Wick a small amount of water around the inside and outside edge of the snake. Use the blending tool to smooth together the ends.

4. Pinch off a small piece of bronze clay, and roll it into a ball. Press the ball flat between your fingers. Pinch one side of the flattened clay to form it into a teardrop shape. This is one flower petal. At the point where the center petal will be positioned, apply slip to the brooch with a paintbrush. Place the flower petal onto the slip. Repeat this step two more times, adding a flower petal on either side of the first.

5. Form a small pinch of bronze clay into a flat triangle that fits under the flower. Add slip to the base of the flower with a paintbrush. Place the small triangle onto the slip, and lightly press it into place. Brush the entire flower with a small amount of water to secure.

6. Place a small ball of bronze clay onto your work surface, and roll it into a thin coil from which to form the flower stem. Starting at the base of the flower, brush a line of slip down the center of the brooch. Place the coil onto the slip, and gently press it into place. Use a wet paintbrush to clean away any excess slip.

7. Roll a small piece of clay into a short log. Press the log flat between your fingers, and then pinch both ends to form points. This is one leaf. Add slip on one side of the flower stem, and press the leaf into place. Repeat this step to form and attach the second leaf.

8. Use your fingers to roll three very small balls of bronze clay. Add a bit of slip to the base of the flower stem, and place the balls onto the slip. Use the paintbrush to remove any excess slip.

9. Roll several more small balls of clay to use as accents around the flower. (I used 14 balls.) Use slip to attach the balls to the brooch. If there is excess slip around the balls, remove it with a paintbrush. Allow the brooch to dry completely.

10. Sand the surface of the brooch with fine sandpaper to remove any fingerprints or brush strokes. Carve lines around the outside edge of the brooch with a carving tool. Also carve the flower petals and leaves to add dimension.

11. Place the brooch in the activated coconut carbon, and fire it in the kiln using the long firing schedule.

12. Rinse the brooch in water and then place it facedown on the soldering block. Position the pin back in the upper third of the paisley and use the torch to solder it onto the brooch. Clean in pickle solution and then rinse thoroughly with water.

13. Polish the brooch in the rotary tumbler. With fine brushes, apply the acrylic model paint onto the paisley brooch. The more color the better! Following the manufacturer's instructions, seal the paint with the spray lacquer.

DESIGNER KNOBS

It seems like whenever I'm looking for a new cabinet door pull, I can't find one that I truly love. In fact, my kitchen cabinets still don't have door pulls because I haven't found a design that I like. Well, now I can have custom door pulls on each cabinet, bringing personality into the room!

NEEDED

Bronze clay kit, page 12

Interestingly patterned button, 1 to 1½ inches (2.5 to 3.8 cm) in diameter

Two-part molding compound

Steel screw, ½ inch (1.3 cm) long, (see tip below)

Steel screw, 1¼ inches (3.2 cm) long

Drying tray (optional)

Finishing and patina supplies of your choice

TIP

A steel or stainless-steel screw won't fuse to the bronze clay when fired. Avoid using any screw that is galvanized. This type of screw reacts with the clay during firing and will fuse to it.

HERE'S HOW

Making the Face of the Cabinet Pull

1. Follow the manufacturer's instructions to mix the two-part molding compound. Press the entire face of a button into the molding compound. It should be pressed in until the compound comes up to the same level as the back side of the button. Allow the mold to cure completely, and then remove the button.

2. Place a lump of bronze clay on your work surface. Use the rolling pin to roll a clay slab that is six cards thick. Place the clay slab onto the mold. Use your fingers to press the clay into the mold, transferring the texture onto the clay.

3. Gently remove the textured clay from the mold, and place it on your work surface. Use a needle tool to cut away any excess clay around the molded surface. Let the clay dry completely.

4. Use an emery file to smooth the edges of the dry, molded clay. Use 400-grit sandpaper to sand the back of the clay completely flat. This element is the face of the pull.

Making the Cabinet Pull Stem

1. Roll a lump of bronze clay into a log that is approximately ¼ inch (6 mm) in diameter. Trim the log so it is ¾ inch (1.9 cm) long.

2. Using a needle tool, pierce a centered pilot hole into one end of the log. The hole should be approximately ¼ inch (6 mm) deep.

3. Gently twist the end of the ½-inch-long (1.3 cm) steel screw into the pilot hole until the head of the screw meets the end of the log. As you rotate the screw into the log, take care not to distort the shape of the clay. Set the log aside to dry naturally.

4. Remove the screw from the dry clay. File both ends of the log completely flat with an emery file.

5. Apply a small amount of olive oil or lubricant to the threads of the 1/2-inch-long (1.3 cm) screw. (This allows the screw to be more easily removed from the clay after firing.) Gently twist the small screw back into the hole, carefully following its interior thread pattern.

Assembling the Cabinet Pull

1. Place the molded clay facedown on your work surface. Find and lightly mark the center of the clay with a pencil. This is where the stem will be placed.

2. Apply a large dollop of thick slip to the pencil mark. Position the end of the stem without the screw perpendicular to the back of the face, and press the stem into the slip. Allow the slip to dry completely.

3. Roll a piece of bronze clay into a thin snake. Wrap the snake around the base of the stem where it's attached to the face. Use a paintbrush to apply a small amount of water to the surface of the snake.

4. Use a blending tool to join the snake and the seam until completely smooth. Place the assembled cabinet pull on a drying tray and let the joint dry completely. Gently sand the dry joint with 400-grit sandpaper.

Firing & Finishing the Pull

1. Place the cabinet pull, with the screw in place, into either activated coconut or coal carbon. Fire the clay in the kiln using the long schedule.

2. Use a screwdriver to remove the screw from the stem of the fired cabinet pull. (It may seem tough to remove the screw, but all it will take is a bit of force and some patience.) Once the screw is removed, replace it with a new, unfired screw that is 1 1/4 inches (3.2 cm) long.

3. Finish the door pull as desired. This project features pulls that have been oxidized, polished, and sealed with lacquer to protect the patina.

TROMPE L'OEIL PENDANT

While the focal point of this piece looks to be stone, it's actually a beautiful piece of paper! The domed resin adds to the illusion. When you're ready for a change, wear the pendant flipped over.

NEEDED

Bronze clay kit, page 12

Oval template, 1½ x 1 inch
  (3.8 x 2.5 cm)

Bronze slip

Cocktail straw

Bronze oxidizer

Polishing cloth or other
  finishing materials

Decorative paper of your choice

White craft glue

Clear epoxy resin

Toothpick

Straight pin

Commercial chain or silk ribbon
  to complement the color in the
  decorative paper

HERE'S HOW

Making the Pendant

1. Place a lump of bronze clay on your work surface. Use the rolling pin to roll a clay slab that is four cards thick.

2. Place the oval template on the bronze clay slab. Use a needle tool to cut out the oval shape. (This is the base of the pendant.) Let the clay oval dry on a drying tray, and then use an emery file to sand its edges.

3. Place a lump of bronze clay on your work surface. Use the rolling pin to roll a clay slab that is three cards thick. Use a tissue blade to cut a strip of clay that is ¼ inch (6 mm) wide and 2½ inches (6.4 cm) long. This strip will form the bezel in the center of the pendant.

4. Form the clay strip into an oval ring that is smaller than the base of the pendant. Overlap the ends of the strip and use water and a blending tool to join the seam of the ring (bezel) together.

5. Using a blending tool, apply bronze slip to the base of the pendant where the bezel will be attached. Place the bezel on top of the slip, and press it into place. Blend in any excess slip with the blending tool. Allow the slip and bezel to dry completely. Inspect the seam between the bezel and base for any gaps. If gaps are found, apply more slip, and let the pendant dry.

6. Sand the top edge of the bezel level with an emery file. The outside edge of the bezel can also be sanded to make the seam smooth.

7. Using small bits of bronze clay, form decorative balls and other embellishments to apply to the outside edge of the bezel. Use bronze slip to adhere each embellishment, and allow the entire assembly to dry.

8. Apply a small amount of lubricant to a cocktail straw. Roll a fresh piece of bronze clay into a thin snake that is 1 inch (2.5 cm) long and ⅛ inch (3 mm) in diameter. Drape the center of the snake over the cocktail straw. Pinch the ends of the clay snake together to form the pendant's bail. Cut away any excess clay with a craft knife.

9. Roll a piece of clay three cards thick. Use a low relief texture to texture the slab of clay. Use the oval template on the textured slab. Apply slip to the entire back of the pendant. Press the oval, texture side out, onto the slip, making sure it's making full connections around the edges. Allow the pendant to dry completely. Sand the edges with an emery file.

10. Using a blending tool, add bronze slip to the top of the back of the pendant. Press the bail into the slip, and blend it into place. Let the slip dry. Once the bail is totally dry, slip it off the straw. File or sand any excess slip off where the bail is attached.

11. Place the pendant in the activated coconut carbon, and fire it in the kiln following the long firing schedule. Finish the fired pendant as desired. For this project, the pendant was oxidized and then polished to bring out its textural details.

Filling & Finishing the Pendant

1. Position the decorative paper face up over the pendant. With a light touch, press the paper into place, making a slight crease where it meets the bezel. Using the crease lines as a guide, cut out a paper oval that fits inside the bezel.

2. Paint a thin layer of the white craft glue on the pendant on the inside of the bezel walls. Press the paper oval into the bezel so it makes full contact with the glue. Paint a layer of the craft glue over the surface of the paper, and let dry. This top layer of glue will seal the paper, preparing it to be capped by the epoxy.

3. Follow the manufacturer's instructions to mix the clear epoxy. Using a toothpick, drizzle the epoxy over the decorative paper. Fill the bezel with the epoxy so it forms a slight dome. As the epoxy cures, watch out for any bubbles that may form. To remove bubbles in the epoxy, poke them with a straight pin. Once any bubbles have been removed, let the epoxy cure completely.

4. String the finished pendant onto a commercial chain or a colorful silk ribbon. No clasp is needed with the latter—just tie the ribbon together to form a pretty little bow at the back of the neck.

MODERN RELIC

Centered at the peak of a layered plateau, the clear sparkle of a single cubic zirconia is the heart of this design. Set this stone directly into the soft clay; it easily tolerates the firing schedule.

NEEDED

Bronze clay tool kit, page 12

Circle templates

Plastic wrap

Tweezers

Cubic zirconia, 5 mm

Cocktail straw

Bronze slip

Cord or chain of your choice

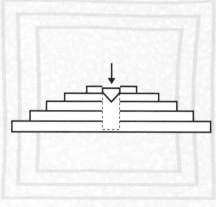

figure 1

HERE'S HOW

1. Place the bronze clay on your work surface. Roll it into a slab that is three cards thick. Using a circle template and a fine needle tool, cut out a circle of clay that is 1½ inches (3.8 cm) in diameter. This will be your base circle. Move this circle to a separate work surface, such as a playing card or a piece of nonstick paper. Having it on a separate surface will make it easier to build the pendant. Cover with plastic wrap.

2. Roll out a slab of bronze clay that is two cards thick. Use the circle template and the fine needle tool to cut out four additional clay circles that measure 1¼, 1, ¾, and ½ inch (3.2, 2.5, 1.9, and 1.3 cm) in diameter. Keep these circles under plastic wrap until you are ready to use them.

3. Use a paintbrush to apply water to the entire surface of the base circle (cut in step 1). Center the 1¼-inch (3.2 cm) circle over the wet base circle. Gently press the two circles together with your fingertip.

4. Wet the top surface of the circle layered in step 3. Center and apply the 1-inch (2.5 cm) circle. Continue the process of wetting, layering, and gently pressing until all circles have been stacked onto each other from largest to smallest. Brush a small amount of water around the circumference of each layered circle. The water will help fill any gaps, ensuring a good bond.

5. Position a cocktail straw over the center of the smallest circle, and cut a hole straight down through all five layers. Pick up the 5 mm cubic zirconia with the tweezers. Place the stone, pointed side down, into the hole. Press the stone down just below the surface of the clay (figure 1). Inspect the stone to make sure it's set evenly. (There's nothing worse than a crooked stone!)

6. Allow the clay to dry completely. Smooth and shape the edges of the dried clay with an emery file.

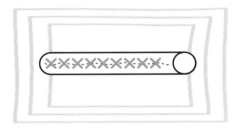

figure 2

7. Cut a cocktail straw about 2 inches (5 cm) long, and apply a bit of olive oil to its surface. Roll out a slab of fresh clay that is two cards thick. Cut a 1-inch-wide (2.5 cm) rectangle from this new slab. Wrap the clay rectangle around the cocktail straw, allowing the ends to overlap. Cut off any excess clay.

8. Use a paintbrush to wet the seam where the clay overlaps. Using a crosshatch motion, blend the seam together with the rubber blending tool (figure 2). Allow the bail to dry completely. Use an emery file to smooth the edges and shape them into angles. Run one side of the tube down the emery file lengthwise to create a flat edge.

9. Make some thick slip and apply it to the flat side of the bail. Press the bail onto the back of the pendant approximately ½ inch (1.3 cm) above the stone. Smooth away any excess slip. Allow the slip to dry completely. Inspect the seam to make sure the bail is making full contact with the pendant. If necessary, add more slip to the seam, smooth into place, and let dry.

10. Place the pendant in the activated coal carbon, and fire it in the kiln on the long firing schedule.

11. Gently rub the fiber pad over the entire surface of the pendant to give it a soft, satin finish. Add the pendant to a cord or chain of your choice.

CRESCENT EARRINGS

Looks can be deceptive. While these lovely earrings may appear weighty, they're really quite lightweight. I used a ping-pong ball to lend them a soft, domed effect.

Bronze clay kit, page 12

Circle template, 1⅝ inches
   (4.1 cm) in diameter

Circle template, 1 inch (2.5 cm)
   in diameter

Ping-pong ball

Drill bit, 1 mm in diameter

Bronze slip

Drying tray (optional)

Rotary tumbler

Stainless steel shot

Burnishing compound

Commercial chain, 4 pieces,
   each 1¼ inches (3.2 cm) long

6 bronze jump rings, 20-gauge,
   4 mm inside diameter wire

Bronze wire, 22-gauge, 6 inches
   (15.2 cm) long

2 garnet briolettes, 6 x 4 mm

2 bronze ear wires, 20-gauge

Note: *Perform each of the following steps twice, once on each earring.*

1. Place a lump of bronze clay on your work surface. Use the rolling pin to roll a clay slab that is four cards thick.

2. Position the 1⅝-inch (4.1 cm) circle template on the rolled clay slab. Use a needle tool to cut out a clay circle.

3. To create the crescent cutaway shape, position the circle template with the 1-inch (2.5 cm) diameter over the top portion of the clay circle. Use a needle tool to cut out the crescent shape.

4. Apply a thin layer of lubricant over the surface of the ping-pong ball. Lift the crescent off your work surface and drape it over the ball. Gently press the crescent to the ball so the clay conforms to its shape. Allow the clay to dry naturally over the ball.

5. Use the emery file to smooth the edges and gently round the corners of the dry clay crescent.

6. Measure and mark two points on the crescent, each approximately 3 mm inside the edge of the tip (figure 1). Use the 1 mm bit to drill a hole at each marked point.

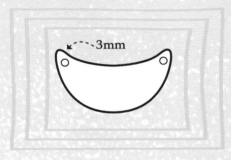

figure 1

7. Roll a thin snake from a small lump of bronze clay. The snake should be approximately 2 mm thick and long enough to wrap around all edges of the crescent.

8. Use a paintbrush to apply a small amount of water to the surface of the snake. Place a sheet of plastic wrap over the snake to keep it moist.

9. Wet all edges of the clay crescent with a damp paintbrush. Remove the moist snake from under the plastic wrap, and gently press it along the edges of the crescent, making full contact. (Don't worry about making fingerprints in the wet clay. These can be sanded away later.) Place the crescent onto the drying tray, and let the snake dry completely.

10. Apply bronze slip to the seam on the back of the crescent, and use a blending tool to smooth the seam. (The slip reinforces the seam and disguises it so it isn't visible from the back.) Place the crescent back onto the dryer, and let the slip dry.

11. Use the fiber sanding pad to sand the areas where slip was applied and to file away any fingerprints left in the snake.

12. Position the earrings vertically in the activated coal carbon, and fire them in the kiln following the standard firing schedule.

13. Place the fired earrings in a rotary tumbler, and tumble them for about 1 hour to produce a bright, high polish finish.

14. Use a jump ring to attach one 1¼-inch (3.2 cm) piece of commercial chain to each hole in both earrings (figure 2).

figure 2

15. For each earring, use another jump ring to connect the two loose chain ends (figure 3).

figure 3

16. Make a wire wrap around one briolette for each earring. Attach the wire-wrapped briolette to the jump ring that holds the two chains together (figure 4).

figure 4

17. To finish, attach one ear wire to the center jump ring on each earring.

SCULPTED FIGURE

Carry this figurine for good luck or just set her on a desk for contemplation. This simple sculpture shows how forms and figures can be made out of bronze clay.

NEEDED

Bronze clay tool kit, page 12

HERE'S HOW

1. Place a large lump of bronze clay on your work surface. Roll the lump into a log that is 1½ inches (3.8 cm) long x ¾ inch (1.9 cm) thick.

2. Pinch each end of the bronze clay log into a tapered blunt point with your fingers. Place the clay onto your work surface, and use the side of your pinky finger to create a waistline just above the center of the log. This curve will give definition between the torso and hips of the figure.

3. Use a blending tool to sculpt details into the torso. The details can be as subtle or as intricate as desired.

4. Using the long side of the needle tool, press lines in the clay figure to form the legs and hip area. Set the figure aside, and allow it to dry naturally. Since this is a thick piece of clay, it will take several hours to dry.

5. Sand the entire surface of the sculpture with a fiber sanding pad.

6. Place the dry clay figure in activated coal carbon, and fire it in the kiln. Important: Because the sculpture is thick, it's best to fire at a slow ramp of 150°F (66°C) per hour and hold it at 1550°F (843°C) for four hours. This will allow the clay to sinter as much as possible.

7. Thoroughly rinse the fired figure to remove any carbon residue. The finish on this project is the natural kiln patina.

SPIRAL BEAD

Use this well-loved, classic bead for necklaces, bracelets, earrings, and more. Roll and fire a large batch to show off bronze clay's stunning straight-from-the-kiln colors.

NEEDED

Bronze clay tool kit, page 12

6 long spacers

Texture sheets (optional)

Cocktail straw

20-gauge bronze wire

Commercial chain

HERE'S HOW

1. Use your hands to roll a medium-sized lump of bronze clay into a log shape. Lightly press the log onto your work surface to flatten it. Position three long spacers on both sides of the log. Roll the bronze into a long strip. If desired, imprint the surface of the clay with a texture sheet. (Remember to lightly oil the textured surface before pressing so the clay won't stick.)

2. Use the tissue blade to cut the clay strip into an isosceles triangle that is 1 inch (2.5 cm) wide with 3 inch (7.6 cm) sides (figure 1). (For those of us whose memory of geometry class is foggy at best, an isosceles triangle has two sides of equal length.) **Note:** *If you textured your clay, turn it over so the texture faces your work surface.*

3. Use a paintbrush to apply water along the center of the clay triangle, avoiding the last ½ inch (1.3 cm) that will be wrapped around the straw.

4. Cut a cocktail straw to approximately 2 inches (5 cm) long. Rub a small amount of oil onto the surface of the straw. Place the straw on the short end of the triangle. Gently pick up the short edge of the clay, and wrap it around the cocktail straw. Continue wrapping until the clay has been completely wrapped around itself (figure 2). Use a paintbrush to wick water onto the bead where the edges meet to ensure a good bond. Let the bead dry completely.

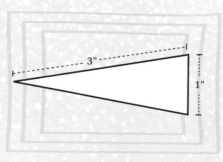

figure 1

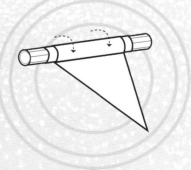

figure 2

5. Remove the cocktail straw from the core of the dry bead. If the straw is being stubborn, slightly twist it as you pull. Using fine sandpaper, smooth the edges of the bead. Smooth inside the hole of the bead with a round needle file.

6. Follow steps 1 through 5 to make as many beads as you wish. Vary the textures of the beads with different texture sheets as desired .

7. Place the beads in the activated coal carbon. Fire them in the kiln using the long firing schedule. No need to finish the surface of the beads—show off the cool colors that occur naturally during firing! String the beads on the cord or chain of your choice.

SACRED HEART

This iconic Milagro symbolizes love for
a person or a deity, or quite literally, the
human heart. The lacy scallops are cleverly
created using an altered drinking straw.

Bronze clay tool kit, page 12

Photocopied template, page 123

Drinking straw

Cocktail straw

Round needle file

Half-round needle file

**Bronze jump ring, 20-gauge,
  ¼ inch (6 mm) in diameter**

Leather cord with clasp

1. Place the bronze clay on your work surface, and roll a slab that is five cards thick. Using the needle tool, cut out a freeform heart shape or use the template provided. With your fingertips, press in the edges of the clay heart to soften them. Set the heart aside to dry completely. Use the emery file to sand and smooth its edge.

2. Roll out a slab of clay that is three cards thick and larger than the heart shape. Apply some water onto the surface of the slab with a paintbrush, and add some slip to the back of the heart. Center the heart over the slab, and press it into place. Wipe away the excess slip with a paintbrush.

3. Cut a drinking straw in half lengthwise to form a semicircle cutter. To create the decorative lace edge, position the cut drinking straw about ¼ inch (6 mm) away from the outside edge of the heart, and cut (figure 1). Continue cutting around the perimeter of the heart, leaving a ¾-inch (1.9 cm) section of clay uncut at the top. This section is where the flames will be placed (figure 2). Use a cocktail straw to create a hole in the center of each semicircle.

figure 1

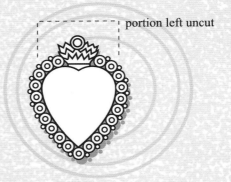

portion left uncut

figure 2

4. Cut a centered semicircle approximately ³⁄₄ inch (1.9 cm) above the top of the heart with the drinking straw cutter. Pierce the center of the semicircle with the cocktail straw.

5. Roll a small pinch of bronze clay into a short pointed snake to create a flame. Brush some slip onto the area above the heart, and press the flame into place. Continue rolling small snakes and pressing them into the slip until the area has been filled. Brush the entire area with slip to ensure that all the flames are well attached.

6. Roll out a small piece of clay that is three cards thick. Cut it ¹⁄₈ inch (3 mm) wide and long enough to cover the bottom portion of the flames. Adhere the strip of clay to the flames by applying a small amount of slip and pressing it into place. Place the pendant aside to dry completely.

7. File the interior edge of each pierced circle with the round needle file. Use the half-round needle file to refine the exterior edges of the lace pattern. Gently sand the entire pendant with the fiber pad. This will give the entire design soft, rounded edges. Sand slowly and carefully—if you sand too fast, the fibers can get tangled in the flames.

8. Place the pendant in the activated coal carbon, and fire it using the long firing schedule. Rinse the pendant after firing to remove any carbon residue. Leave the kiln patina on the pendant. Add a jump ring to the bail, and string it onto a leather cord.

ELLIPSE EARRINGS

Sometimes it's the most effortless designs that are most appreciated. This project removes all the clutter that is sometimes found in metal clay designs and lets the metal speak for itself.

NEEDED

Bronze clay tool kit, page 12

Oval template

Circle template

Round needle file

Half-round needle file

Rotary tumbler with steel shot

Ear wires of your choice

Two jump rings

HERE'S HOW

1. Place the bronze clay on your work surface, and roll a smooth slab that is four cards thick. Use the oval template and a needle tool to cut out two identical ovals from the slab.

2. Select a circle from the template that fits inside the lower third of the clay oval. Position the template on one clay oval, and use the needle tool to cut out the interior circle. Cut out the interior circle from the second oval. Make a pilot hole at the top of each earring with the needle tool. Let both earrings dry completely.

3. With the emery file, sand the outside edge of the earrings. Use a half-round needle file to smooth the interior edge. Enlarge the pilot hole at the top of each earring with the round needle file.

4. Place the earrings in the activated coconut carbon, and fire them in the kiln using the short firing schedule.

5. Place the fired earrings in a rotary tumbler with steel shot, and tumble them up to two hours.

6. Attach each completed earring to an ear wire.

ARTFUL BUTTONS

Buttons have always been some of my favorites. Growing up as a daughter of a seamstress, my mom had tins full of fantastic old buttons that I would play with for hours.

NEEDED

- **Bronze clay kit, page 12**
- **Rubber stamps of your choice**
- **Circle template, 1½ inches (3.8 cm)**
- **Ping-pong ball**
- **Drill bit, 1.5 mm in diameter**
- **Bronze slip**
- **Rotary tumbler, optional**
- **Liver of sulfur or other patina, optional**

HERE'S HOW

1. Place a lump of bronze clay on your work surface. Use the rolling pin to roll a slab that is five cards thick. Lubricate a rubber stamp, and press it into the surface of the clay slab.

2. Position the circle template over the stamped clay, and center the template over the design area you like most. Using a needle tool, cut out the circle of stamped clay.

3. Apply a small amount of oil or lubricant to the surface of the ping-pong ball. Place the clay circle onto the ball, and gently press it onto the surface. Set the ball aside, and allow the clay to dry completely.

4. Use an emery file to sand and smooth the edges of the dry, domed clay (the button).

5. Place a lump of bronze clay on your work surface. Use the rolling pin to roll a slab that is six cards thick. Cut a strip from the slab that is ⅜ x ½ inch (1 x 1.3 cm). This strip will be the shank of the button. Let the piece dry completely.

6. Use an emery file to smooth the long sides of the dry clay strip and to round one end (figure 1).

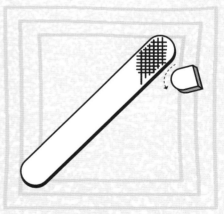

figure 1

figure 2

7. Measure and mark a centered point on the rounded end of the strip that is approximately 3 mm away from the end. Use the drill bit to make a hole at the marked point.

8. Apply a dollop of bronze slip in the center of the back of the button. Form a small ball of bronze clay, and press it into the slip. If the button back is flat, you can skip this step.

9. Press the narrow, flat end of the shank into the lump of clay or slip on the back of the button (figure 2). Use the blending tool with a small amount of water to blend the clay around the shank. Allow the clay to dry.

10. Use sandpaper to smooth the seams where the shank was attached to the button.

11. Repeat steps 1 through 10 to make as many buttons as desired.

12. Place the button/buttons faceup in the activated coconut carbon, and fire the clay in the kiln using the long firing schedule.

13. Finish the fired clay buttons as desired. The featured buttons were polished in a rotary tumbler, and then oxidized to bring out the textural details.

SPIRIT WIND CHIME

The affordability of bronze clay allows you to create décor items for both inside and outside your home. You'll find the teardrop-shaped bronze pieces make light, pleasing chimes when brushed with the hand or a breeze.

Bronze clay kit, page 12

Wind chime base template,
    page 123

Circle cutter, ½ inch (1.3 cm)
    in diameter

Circle cutter, ¼ inch (6 mm)
    in diameter

Teardrop appliqué template,
    page 123

Bronze slip

Carving tools

Drill bit, 1 mm in diameter

Chime template, page 123

Beading wire

Crimp beads

Assorted beads

Making the Wind Chime Base

1. Photocopy the template for the wind chime base. Cut out the template with scissors.

2. Place a large lump of bronze clay on your work surface. Use the rolling pin to roll the clay into a slab that is four cards thick. Place the wind chime base template on the clay slab, and use a craft knife to cut out the clay. Let the clay dry naturally to avoid any warping or cracking.

3. To make the embellishments, place a lump of bronze clay on your work surface. Use the rolling pin to roll the clay into a slab that is three cards thick. Using the ½-inch (1.3 cm) circle cutter, cut out one clay circle and put it under plastic wrap to keep the circle moist. Using the ¼-inch (6 mm) circle cutter, cut out seven clay circles and put them under the plastic wrap.

4. Use a craft knife to cut out seven thin teardrop shapes from the clay slab. Make each teardrop shape approximately 1 inch (2.5 cm) long by ½ inch (1.3 cm) wide at the widest point of the drop, or photocopy and use the teardrop appliqué template provided. Place the teardrop shapes under the plastic wrap with the circle.

5. Use a paintbrush to lightly wet the wind chime base in the area where the embellishments will be placed. Add some bronze slip to the moistened area. Arrange the ½-inch (1.3 cm) clay circle and the thin teardrops onto the slip. Center and layer one ¼-inch (6 mm) clay circle on top of each teardrop shape. Wick water around the edges of each embellishment with the paintbrush, and smooth away any excess slip.

6. Roll 12 small bronze clay balls of equal size. Using slip, apply a set of three small balls at the top, the bottom, and on both sides of the wind chime base. Smooth away any excess slip with a blending tool. Set the wind chime base aside. Allow the embellishments and bronze slip to dry completely.

7. Use a pencil to draw simple, decorative lines on the surface of the wind chime base. Use a carving tool to carve the lines that were sketched onto the base and create texture.

8. With a craft knife, whittle away the center of each flat circle appliqué to create negative space.

9. Using the 1 mm bit, drill two equally spaced and level holes near the top edge of the wind chime base. Drill seven equally spaced holes near the bottom edge of the base (figure 1).

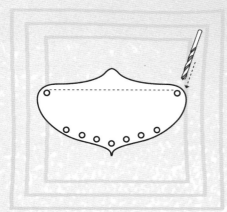

figure 1

Making the Chimes

1. Place a lump of bronze clay on your work surface. Use the rolling pin to roll the clay into a slab that is five cards thick.

2. Cut seven teardrop shapes out of the bronze clay slab, each measuring 1½ inches (3.8 cm) long by ¾ inch (1.9 cm) wide (or photocopy and use the chime template provided.) Place each clay chime onto the drying tray, and let dry.

3. Roll a small pinch of clay into a ball shape. Add a small amount of slip to the center of one of the teardrops. Press the ball shape into the slip. Roll a small pinch of clay about the size of a peppercorn between your fingers to form a small log. Pinch it flat, and form it into a leaf shape. Add a small amount of slip to the top side of the ball embellishment. Press the small leaf shape into the slip. Make two more small leaf shapes, and press them into the slip. Allow the slip to dry. The chimes can also be carved for added detail.

4. Using the 1 mm bit, drill one centered hole approximately 3 mm inside the top edge of each chime.

Finishing & Assembling the Wind Chimes

1. Use an emery file to smooth the edges of the wind chime base as well as each chime. Sand the entire surface of each piece, and soften all edges with a fiber sanding pad.

2. Position the base and chimes vertically in activated coconut carbon inside the firing container, and, using the long firing schedule, fire the clay in the kiln. (If the base or chimes warp during firing, place them on a steel bench block and flatten them with a mallet.)

3. Finish the fired clay elements as desired. (For this project, a liver-of-sulfur patina was applied to bring out the details of the carving and embellishments. Then, polishing wheels were used to shine the high surfaces.)

4. String a chime onto a 7-inch (17.8 cm) length of beading wire, and secure the chime with a crimp bead. String approximately 4½ inches (11.4 cm) of decorative beads onto the wire in the pattern of your choice. Feed the free end of the beading wire through one hole in the bottom edge of the chime base. Secure the beaded chime wire to the base with a second crimp bead. Repeat this step for each remaining bronze chime.

5. String a bead or beads of your choice onto a 2-inch (5 cm) eye pin. Feed the free end of the eye pin through one hole at the top edge of the chime base. With needle-nose pliers, bend a loop in the wire to secure the eye pin to the chime base. Cut off any excess wire. Repeat this step for the second hole at the top of the base.

6. To create a hanging device, string the cord of your choice through both eye pin loops, and tie to secure.

TABLET EARRINGS

Experiment with different textures to sharpen your repertoire and get a look that's all your own. Then make one or several pairs of simple earrings to wear or share.

NEEDED

Bronze clay tool kit, page 12

2 beads, each 4 mm

2 gold-filled eye pins, each 1 inch (2.5 cm) long

Round-nose pliers

2 gold-filled ear wires

Round needle file

HERE'S HOW

1. Place a lump of clay that is the size of a large coin on your work surface. Roll the clay into a slab that is four cards thick.

2. Use the edge of a playing card to gently press horizontal lines in the surface of the clay. Don't press too hard, or you might cut through the clay or create a weak spot.

3. With the tissue blade, cut two rectangles from the textured slab, each 2 inches (5 cm) long by ¾ inch (1.9 cm) wide.

4. Use a needle tool to pilot a small, centered hole near the top of each strip of clay. (Once the clay is completely dry, these holes will be widened with a needle file.) Let both pieces of clay dry completely.

5. Use an emery file to smooth the edges and round the corners of each earring. Smooth out the hole at the top of each earring with a round needle file.

6. Place the earrings in the activated coal carbon, and fire them in the kiln following the short firing schedule.

7. Rinse the fired earrings in water to remove any remaining carbon. Use several grits of polishing papers to get a high polish. Start with 400-grit paper and work your way through finer grits, finishing with 8000-grit paper.

8. Add one bead to each of the gold-filled eye pins. Using round-nose pliers, make an eye at the end of each pin. Attach the beaded eye pins to the earrings. Add an ear wire to each earring to complete the pair.

INCENSE VESSEL

The aroma of incense can transport you to serene and exotic places. This delicate bowl neatly catches the ashes from either the stick or cone variety.

NEEDED

Bronze clay tool kit, page 12

Ping-pong ball

Circle template, 2 inches (5 cm) in diameter

Circle cutter, ½ inch (1.3 cm) in diameter

Bronze slip

Drinking straw

Drill bit, 1.5 mm in diameter

HERE'S HOW

1. Apply a thin layer of oil to the ping-pong ball. (This helps prevent the clay, as it is being formed and dried, from sticking to the ball.) Roll the bronze clay into a slab that is four cards thick. Place the circle template on the slab, and use the needle tool to cut a circle that is 2 inches (5 cm) in diameter.

2. To form the bowl of the incense holder, lift the circle of clay off the work surface and place it onto the ping-pong ball. Gently press the clay, molding it to the ball's shape, while supporting the ball so it doesn't roll away. Let the clay dry completely.

3. Remove the dry clay from the ball. Use the emery file to sand the edges of the bowl. Find the center of the bowl on its bottom surface, and mark this point with a pencil.

4. Roll a slab of clay that is 12 cards thick. Cut a ½-inch (1.3 cm) circle with the circle cutter. Using slip, attach the thick circle to the bottom of the bowl at the center point marked in step 3. Set the bowl aside, and let the circle dry. Smooth the edges and bottom of the dried circle with the emery file.

5. Roll a slab of clay that is three cards thick. Cut eight circles with the ½-inch (1.3 cm) circle cutter. Use the drinking straw to cut a hole in the center of each circle, transforming the circles into rings. Place the rings under plastic wrap to keep them moist.

6. Wet the outside and inside rim of the incense bowl. Center one of the rings (made in step 5) on the rim of the bowl. Fold the ring over the rim of the bowl, pressing it on the inside and outside of the rim. Run a wet paintbrush around the inside and outside of each ring to ensure a good connection. Repeat this step to attach the remaining rings.

7. Allow the rings to dry completely. Use the fiber pad to soften the edges of the rings on the rim of the bowl. Drill a hole in the center of the bowl with the drill bit, taking care not to drill all the way through the base of the bowl. (This depression will hold the incense sticks in place as they are burned.)

8. Vertically place the incense holder in the activated coconut carbon. Fire the piece in the kiln using the long firing schedule. Rinse the incense holder in water to remove any residue left by the carbon. Leave the kiln patina on the surface of the bronze for an antique look. The natural patina of the bronze will change over time as incense is burned in the holder.

116

DIAMOND EARRINGS

I like the dramatic contrast of the bronze center strip on these earrings against the beautiful blue-green patina—a finish that can only be achieved with bronze clay.

NEEDED

Bronze clay tool kit, page 12

Low-relief texture sheet

Photocopied template, page 122

Two ping-pong balls or other round form

Blue-green oxidizing solution

Gold-filled ear wires, commercial or handmade

Round needle file

Two jmp rings, 20-gauge, 5mm in diameter

HERE'S HOW

1. Place the bronze clay on the work surface. Use the rolling pin to roll the clay into a slab that is four cards thick. Lightly press a low-relief texture sheet onto the surface of the clay.

2. Place the two diamond-shaped templates on top of the clay. Use a craft knife to cut out the diamond shapes. Drape each metal clay shape over a round form, such as a ping-pong ball or lightbulb.

3. Roll out a slab of bronze clay that is two cards thick. Use the tissue blade to cut out two clay strips, each ¼ inch (6 mm) wide and long enough to run the length of the diamond forms from tip to tip.

4. With a wet paintbrush, add some water lengthwise down the center of one diamond form. Place one strip of clay on the wet area. Lightly press the strip down, making sure it sticks. Paint a bit of water along the edges of the strip. Use a craft knife to trim the ends of each strip to match the diamond shape. Repeat this step to add a strip to the second earring.

5. Use the needle tool to pilot a hole centered at the top of each earring.

6. Once dry, use the emery files to sand the edges of the earrings smooth. Enlarge the pilot holes with the round needle file.

7. When loading the firing container, place the earrings in the activated coal carbon vertically. This will help keep the curve in the earrings. Fire the earrings in the kiln following the long firing schedule.

8. Carefully clean the fired earrings. Following the manufacturer's instructions, place the fired earrings in a blue-green oxidizing solution. Once the earrings have been oxidized, use some polishing paper to polish the center strip to a high shine. Attach the ear wires to complete the earrings.

ATHENA COLLAR

Sixteen textured triangles form the basis of this piece. Each wire-wrapped link is so simple yet so attractive when joined en masse.

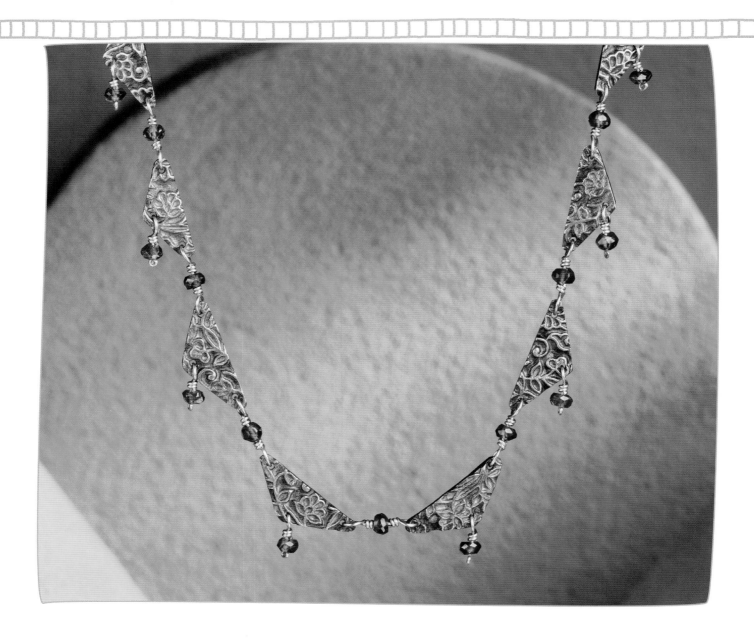

NEEDED

Bronze clay kit, page 12

Texture sheet of your choice

Drill bit, 1 mm in diameter

Plastic or rawhide mallet

Bench block

Bronze oxidizer

54 inches (137.2 cm) of gold-filled wire, 22-gauge

33 faceted garnet beads, 4 mm

5 inches (12.7 cm) of gold-filled wire, 20-gauge (for clasp)

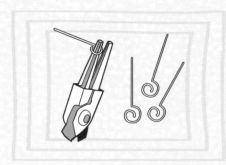

figure 1

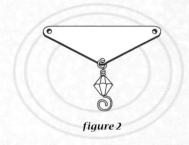

figure 2

HERE'S HOW

1. Place a lump of bronze clay on your work surface. Use the rolling pin to roll a clay slab that is five cards thick.

2. Lubricate the texture sheet, place it onto the clay slab, and texture the entire surface area.

3. Use a craft knife to cut 16 triangles from the bronze clay slab, each 1 inch (2.5 cm) long by ½ inch (1.3 cm) wide at the widest point. Place all the clay triangles on the drying tray. Let them dry completely.

4. Use an emery file to sand the edges of each clay triangle and to round each point.

5. Rub the fiber sanding pad across the surface and the edges of each triangle to give each component a smooth, worn look.

6. In each corner of all triangles, measure and mark a point that is approximately 2 mm inside the edge. Use the bit to drill a hole at each marked point. (The holes are very close to the edges, so apply light, even pressure to the bit so the clay doesn't crack.)

7. Position the clay triangles in activated coconut carbon, and then fire them in the kiln following the short firing schedule. (If the triangles warp during firing, place them on a bench block and hammer them flat with a mallet.)

8. Oxidize each triangle so the texture becomes nice and dark. Use a polishing cloth to remove oxidation from the high points of the texture as well as from the back of each triangle.

9. Use round-nose pliers to make 16 spiral 1-inch (2.5 cm) head pins from the 22-gauge, gold-filled wire (figure 1). Place one faceted garnet bead on each head pin.

10. Use a wire wrap to connect one beaded head pin to the bottom point of each triangle (figure 2).

11. Use the 22-gauge wire to wrap each component together, using a bead as a spacer between each triangle (figure 3). Make a hook-and-eye clasp out of the 20-gauge wire, and attach it to the ends of the necklace.

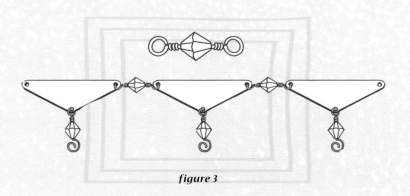

figure 3

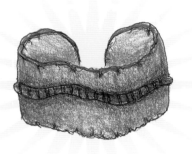

OLYMPIAN CUFF

The irregularity of this cuff makes it look like a find from an archeological dig. The blue-green patina of the raised rope design that adds to the feeling of antiquity is achieved through ammonia fuming.

NEEDED

Bronze clay kit, page 12

Bronze slip

Oval bracelet mandrel, wooden

Flat-edged blending tool

Plastic or rawhide mallet

Ammonia

Salt

Flexible shaft or motorized rotary tool with polishing wheels

Lacquer

HERE'S HOW

1. On the work surface, roll a fresh piece of bronze clay into a log that is approximately 2 inches (5 cm) long with a ¾-inch (1.9 cm) diameter. Gently flatten the log with your fingers.

2. Roll the flattened log into a slab that is four cards thick and 7 inches (17.8 cm) long. As the clay is being rolled, natural cracks will form in its edges.

3. Wrap the bracelet mandrel in plastic wrap. Wrap the rolled clay around the mandrel so that the ends of the bracelet are approximately ½ inch (1.3 cm) apart. Allow the bracelet to partially dry on the mandrel.

4. Gently slip the plastic wrap off the mandrel. As the plastic wrap is being removed, the bracelet will go with it. Remove the plastic wrap from inside the bracelet. Set the bracelet aside to dry naturally.

5. Roll a bronze clay snake that is 7 inches (17.8 cm) long by ⅛ inch (3 mm) thick. Wet a paintbrush with water, and brush it over the surface of the snake. Cover the clay snake with plastic wrap to keep it moist.

6. Using the blending tool, apply a generous amount of thick slip down the center of the dried bracelet from end to end.

7. Press the thin clay snake onto the slip on the bracelet. (The snake doesn't need to be perfectly centered on the bracelet. The bracelet looks even better if the snake is more of a meandering line.) Use a damp paintbrush to smooth any excess slip around the edges of the snake.

8. Using the end of the flat-edged blending tool, press lines into the snake to add texture. Allow the bracelet to dry completely. Inspect the seam to make sure the snake is in complete contact with the bracelet. If needed, apply more slip to ensure a good bond.

9. Use the fiber sanding pad to sand all edges of the bracelet smooth and to soften and round it edges.

10. Place the bracelet in the activated coconut carbon, and then fire it in the kiln following the long firing schedule. Thoroughly rinse the fired bracelet so it is clean of any carbon particles.

11. Place the fired bracelet onto the oval mandrel. Use a plastic or rawhide mallet to shape it into a cuff. (Most cuff bracelets have a 1-inch [2.5 cm] opening between the ends.)

12. Pack the salt onto the snake accent on the bracelet. Place a small bowl of ammonia into a sealable container. Put the bracelet into the container with the bowl, and seal (see page 25 for more information). Allow the bracelet to fume for a few days to produce a blue-green patina where the salt has been packed. Remove the bracelet from the container, and rinse away the salt with water.

13. Use a flexible shaft or motorized rotary tool with polishing wheel attachments to polish the bracelet, avoiding the patinated surface.

14. To prevent the patina from changing color, seal the bronze with lacquer. Also apply the lacquer to the inside of the cuff. This will inhibit skin from turning green as the bracelet is worn.

BRONZE
METAL CLAY
TEMPLATES

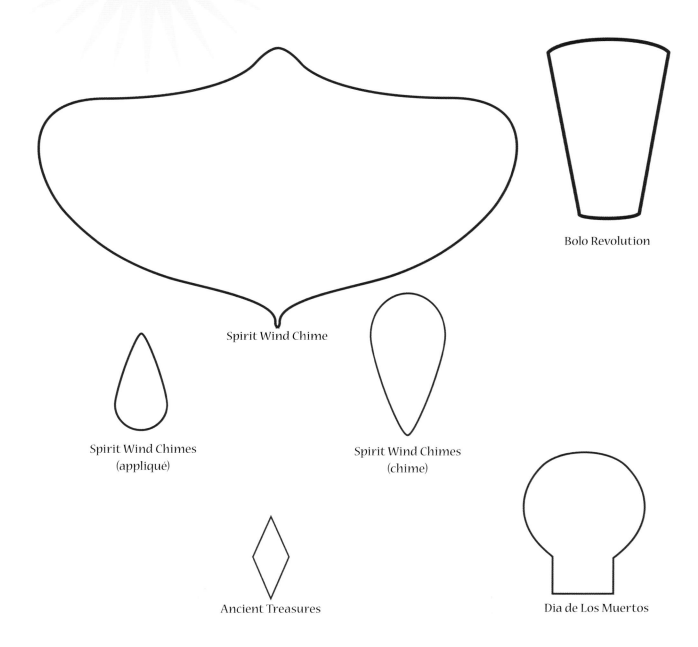

Bolo Revolution

Spirit Wind Chime

Spirit Wind Chimes
(appliqué)

Spirit Wind Chimes
(chime)

Ancient Treasures

Dia de Los Muertos

(templates are actual size)

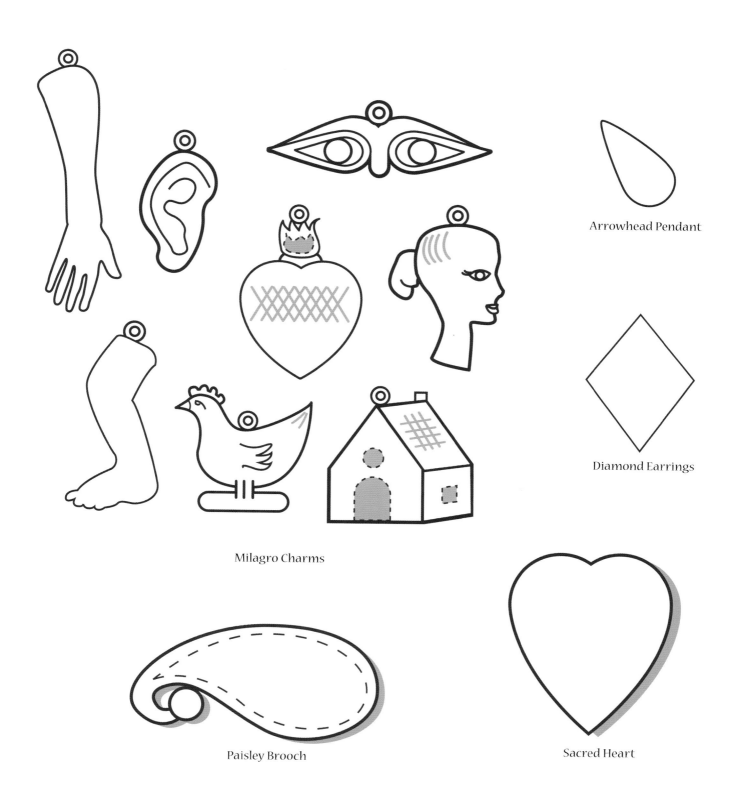

Arrowhead Pendant

Diamond Earrings

Milagro Charms

Paisley Brooch

Sacred Heart

(templates are actual size)

ABOUT THE AUTHOR

Yvonne M. Padilla has been making things since she was itty bitty. She used her sewing skills (Mom taught her how) to turn her red Converse sneakers into ruby slippers; she used a hammer, a box of nails, and the block of wood Dad gave her to create a collection of "nail art"; she drafted her own patterns so that one day she could have her own clothing line; and she hung dollhouse miniatures from ear wires (the farm animals were her favorites) and started selling them to friends at school.

Today, Yvonne is a member of Rio Grande's Technical Support team, an accomplished PMC artist and jeweler, and an enthusiastic instructor. She is self-taught in many art and crafting techniques—jewelry and beyond—and spends countless hours experimenting with new materials and processes.

Yvonne has taught numerous classes at Rio Grande's Albuquerque, New Mexico, facility; Rio Grande's Catalog in Motion; Bead & Button; and Bead Fest, igniting the interest of hundreds of PMC, stringing, and jewelry-making students. She has presented at the bi-annual PMC Conference and was a guest presenter for the New Mexico Bead Society.

Yvonne is one of the first artists in the United States to work with Bronze Clay. "It's been an adventure working with such a new medium," she says. "One that seems so familiar to work with but at the same time is worlds apart from other types of clay."

When Yvonne is not making jewelry or teaching, she crochets, embroiders, sews, is an avid 24 and Comedy Central fan, and loves to host parties. "But really," she says, "my life totally revolves around my dog." Yvonne lives in Rio Rancho, New Mexico, with her husband, Trafford, and their chihuahua, Shadow.

ACKNOWLEDGMENTS

I would first like to thank Bill and Lacey Ann Struve for creating bronze clay. Your tenacity to perfect bronze clay has paid off. Thank you to Kevin Whitmore for all your efforts that brought this product to artists around the world.

Cece Wire, Diana Montoya, and Spencer Baum, thank you for taking the time to listen to my ideas and for the enthusiasm and encouragement you gave me to pursue writing this book. My editors, Linda Kopp and Marthe Le Van, and everyone at Lark, thank you for your guidance and tough love. Thank you to Catherine Silver and Jim Erskine (www.thearchnc.com) for all your help with the Earth Clay Plaster. The backdrops for the photos are beautiful!

All the amazing artists who have contributed to this book, I am honored that you have so generously shared your work with the world.

To the amazing crew at Rio Grande – Gail Phillip, Virginia Dickson, and Sarita Vinje, thank you for all your help with every bronze clay class. Patti Sowell, Mark "Donna" Nelson, Sessin Durgham, Ronnie Mares, Phillip Scott, Ronnie Mares, Patrick Sage, Alex Verdooren, Maria Baca, and Thackeray Taylor, thank you for giving me your opinions, encouragement, technical support, and the occasional hard time.

To all my friends and family, thank you for your constant support and knowing when to tell me to chill out. Shelby Chant, Faith Tomlinson, Meredith Ryan-Smith, Carrie Butler, Tara Anderson, Mary Gallegos, Chris Nigh, and Wes Smith, I love you all. James Gros, I love your artwork. My parents, Donald and Jennie Padilla, thank you for always encouraging every artistic avenue I ever wanted to pursue. To the Treadwell family, you are the best in-laws I could have ever hoped for.

And finally my deepest thanks to my loving husband, Trafford Treadwell. Thank you for your support throughout this whole crazy adventure. I couldn't imagine doing this project without you by my side.

INDEX

INDEX OF GALLERY ARTISTS

Like working with metal clay?
Try these other inspiring titles from Lark Books.

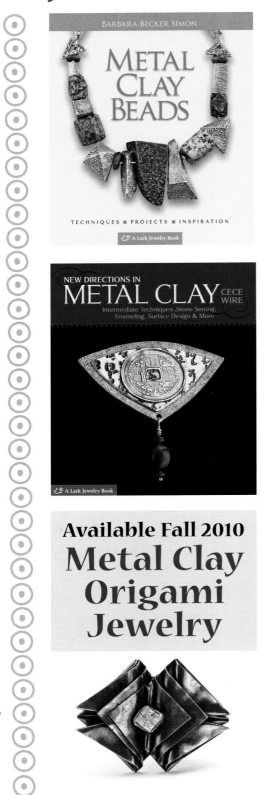

Metal Clay Beads
In this unique, comprehensive reference, Barbara Becker Simon treats readers to 22 outstanding metal clay bead projects, including an introductory section filled with all the fundamentals: forming and joining clay; firing and finishing; adding gemstones, glass, and other objects; using molded and carved texture plates; developing rich patinas; and much more. ISBN - 978-1600590252

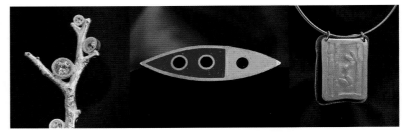

Now in Paperback: New Directions in Metal Clay
A leader in the metal clay community, CeCe Wire details all the newest innovations and clays, as well as the basics for beginners. She includes every form and formula, plus an extensive array of cutting-edge techniques that range from stone-setting and surface embellishment to enameling methods such as champlevé, inlaying with epoxy resin, and silk screening. ISBN - 978-1600595462

Available Fall 2010
Metal Clay Origami Jewelry

Metal Clay Origami Jewelry: 25 Contemporary Projects
Author Sara Jayne Cole takes a traditional paper art and applies it to one of the most innovative jewelry materials on the market: metal clay sheet. After a brief introduction to basic folding techniques and tips for working with this versatile material, Sara Jayne shows readers how to make 25 modern and unique projects with easy step-by-step photo instructions and assembly information.
ISBN - 978-1600595332